PRAISE FOR *B.A.(*

"B.A.G.H.D.A.D Yoga *is an inspirational war story.*
It takes the reader on a journey like no other: basic
training, meditation, a war zone, yoga. LTC Michele
Spencer connects us with her path of a peaceful warrior
through her experience as a combat veteran. She
beautifully weaves together the foundations of yoga
while showing us what it means to experience them. In
this beautiful memoir, the reader gets an inside look at
the life of a Soldier, at war. It's an organic, honest, and
vivid portrayal of her life. How blessed we are to share
this journey with her, as her shift in consciousness takes
us from fear to love, and from war to peace."
Gina Garcia, founder of Yoga Across America

"*Yoga and mindfulness meditation are increasingly*
being considered effective complementary therapies for
treatment of anxiety disorders like insomnia, depression
and PTSD. B.A.G.H.D.A.D Yoga *illustrates how one*
Soldier successfully combined a military career with a
yoga practice, and how this helped her get through and
recover from the stress and pressures of serving with the
Multi-National Security Transition Command in the
heart of Baghdad, Iraq. B.A.G.H.D.A.D. Yoga *ends on*
a particularly interesting note when Michele Spencer
observes the sentencing of Saddam Hussein."
Rob Schware, co-founder and executive director,
The Give Back Yoga Foundation

"*A powerful read by a caring combat veteran who candidly shares with us the daily stressors of combat, deployment, and life! The reader trusts Michele to personally guide us through the B.A.G.H.D.A.D. Yoga journey, realizing every step of the way that her personal story is a triumph for us all. Michele shows us that 'we matter' as we travel this road of personal awareness.*"

LTC Greg Moye, FA, USAR

"*LTC Spencer has undertaken the courageous task of relating her story of how she was able to interweave her experiences during military service with that of embracing and living a number of universal spirtual principals while doing so. Many who profess to be 'spiritual beings' (which, by the way, we all are) may find this difficult to reconcile. Upon reading B.A.G.H.D.A.D. Yoga, we are all transformed by the honesty with which Michele tells her story. There are times when you will smile, when you will say 'Go Girl,' or when you will simply reflect on your life to ask yourself 'What more can I do?' It is a wonderful, insightful, soul-touching piece of work that will inspire us all to want to do just a little better.*"

Brenda Chambliss, attorney

"*Inspirational . . . In B.A.G.H.D.A.D. Yoga, Michele weaves the asanas of Yoga, the challenges of war, and the autobiographical story of her life into a thought-provoking narrative that recognizes and honors the warrior in each of us, demanding it to come fearlessly forward. You will laugh, cry, stop and think and wonder why. It is a gift to those who read it and a challenge to all of us to wake up and live our lives, expressing who we are to the fullest."*

Diane Juray, acupuncturist, yogini, and traveler

"A perspective never heard from a war zone and a powerful example of a woman's journey to wholeness through yoga. Michele shows authentic care and concern for her Soldiers and her mission: peace and hope. I am proud to serve in her company of peaceful warriors!"

Vanessa Meade, U.S. Army/Gulf War veteran, founder of Alaska Veterans Organization for Women (A.V.O.W.)

"Michele captured a love story; love for God, Duty, Honor, Country. It is the love ideal that we ALL are 'powerful beyond measure' and that we are meant to share it with the world . . . wherever we are. No matter the profession, we must be the change we seek!"

OEF/OIF veteran

"Amazing! Michele vividly describes a journey of courage, love, joy, trials, and triumphs. Her journey is remarkable and inspirational; you cannot help but want to Show Up and Deliver every day of your life! Thank you for sharing your journey . . . It undeniably helps me along mine."

LTC Andrea McCollum, OIF veteran

"Michele Spencer paints images that draw you into her amazing story. Veterans and non-veterans alike will connect with the struggles, victories, and lessons of this extraordinary story."

Gina Anderson, MAJ (ret), OIF 2005–2007

Michele . . . has weaved together an insightful book . . . one of TRUE encouragement. She reveals an intimate peak on her own transformation but also embraces you with comfort and challenge. This motivation encourages me to step away from my FEAR . . . and operate from a 'healing open heart.' She encourages us that THIS transformation dwells in us all. She makes you want to be a better person . . . one of SERVICE!

Leslie Gates, BFF, military grandmom

This book is a hybrid in the author/artist's quest to play her part in saving the earth and the soul. She blends narrative, poetry and cliché in a very innovative, creative and unique style that works. The energy of the book wells up from the replenishable soul of an army "soul-dier" . . . Michele brings up moral and ethical issues about how we spend our money, how we treat women and the poor, the perplexity of the military industrial complex, and racism, to name a few.

Ron Camarda, Military Writers Society of America

B.A.G.H.D.A.D.
Yoga

Namaste Lori
May ya be inspired
by my journey and
continue to thrive in yours!
Thank you for YOUR
service - Follow Your Bliss!

Live y Love
Mile

B.A.G.H.D.A.D.

A Shift in Consciousness:
Fear to Love, War to Peace

Michele M. Spencer

Live 4 Love, LLC • Rancho Murieta, California

Live 4 Love, LLC
www.liv4lov.com

First edition, 2012
ISBN 978-0-9886492-0-0

Excerpt from *Zen: The Path of Paradox* by Osho reprinted with permission of Osho International Foundation, www.osho.com/copyrights; excerpt from *The Other Side of War: Women's Stories of Survival and Hope* by Zainab Salbi reprinted with permission; "What is happening" by Alice Walker reprinted with permission.

Design by Williams Writing, Editing & Design
Cover photo & back cover photo composition by Ashlee Nichols
Author photo by Ron Littlejohn
Spine illustration by John Spencer

The views and opinions expressed in this book are solely those of the author and do not reflect the views and opinions of the Army, the Department of Defense, or the United States government.

Note to Readers: This book is intended to be an informational guide and is not meant to treat, diagnose, or prescribe. Always consult with a qualified health care professional regarding any medical condition or symptoms. Neither the author nor the publisher accepts any responsibility for your health or how you choose to use the information contained in this book.

To my parents, John and Geraldine Spencer,
for they gave me wings,
to my brothers Michael and John, who pushed me,
and to my sons Miguel and Clayton Carodine;
I am your wind . . . fly high, soar and enjoy the
journey!

And for ALL my SOUL-diers:
Soldiers, Sailors, Airmen, Marines, and Veterans —
Warriors — Thank YOU for your Service!

On War

A man of peace is not a pacifist, a man of peace is
    simply a pool of silence.
He pulsates a new kind of energy into the world, he
    sings a new kind of song.
He lives in a totally new way, his very way of life is
    that of grace, that of prayer, that of compassion.
Whomever he touches, he creates more love-energy.
The man of peace is creative.
He is not against war, because to be against any thing
    is to be at war.
He is not against war; he simply understands why war
    exists.
And out of that understanding he becomes peaceful.
Only when there are many people who are pools of
    peace, silence, and understanding, will war dis-
    appear.

Osho

Service is the rent we pay for the privilege of living on this earth.

Shirley Chisholm

CONTENTS

Foreword

Yoga. There are many definitions of this simple four-letter word, with the most common being union, but union of what exactly? We live in a world comprised of opposites: day/night, winter/summer, male/female, front/back, happiness/sadness, up/down, inhale/exhale, right/left, rich/poor, birth/death, and on and on with an endless list of opposing forces at play within the realms of this world in which we reside. Yoga seeks to make sense of the seemingly senseless and to bring peace and clarity in the midst of chaos.

Michele Spencer takes us on a journey into the very depths of this struggle deep into the heart of the warrior and the soul of the seeker. Personal growth and the path toward inner awareness, strength, and peace are rarely traveled in a straight line.

Michele has, however, crafted *B.A.G.H.D.A.D. Yoga* into a well-structured, practical, informative, humorous, and enlightening book that demonstrates just how yoga may be utilized in a very raw and real way to help create balance within our own life struggles and upon the battlefields of real-life existence and to help us all feel a little Piece of Peace while following our heart, building our dreams and treading our own special path of life.

Whether you are new to yoga, a seasoned practitioner, or simply a curious individual looking for inspiration, this book is filled with useful insights for all!

David Swenson

Acknowledgments

I am ever so grateful to be in-spirited with the Divine to create this snapshot of my life. Writing was healing; and every fiber of my being needed to communicate that globally we must heal from war, chaos, destruction, economic disparity — trauma and pain from the separation from the truth of our interconnectedness. That there is another way with compassion, cooperation, personal empowerment, global sustainability, and the mighty power of love!

I could not have written this without my own connected believers. Rita Cusak, a holistic practitioner, gave me hope by not laughing at me and reading my very rough, rough draft; Zaji of Creative Ankh shaped and smoothed the edges while Lisa Rhodes became an endearing friend and warrior in her own right as she coached me to continue when I wanted to give up. And then Sandra Williams midwifed *B.A.G.H.D.A.D. Yoga*; her expertise, her grace, kept us alive and together we birthed a story I pray will not only shift the world to see our military in a different light, but also inspire others on their own transformative journey. The amazing David Swenson blessed me with a poignant foreword that sends chills and makes me effervescent.

So many people have influenced my life — even the critics and skeptics — I apologize if I did not name you . . . I do greatly appreciate your gift. There are a host of fellow colleagues and friends that I absolutely adore and that inspired me and gave me strength to endure: Al "Rufus", Andrea, Andre, Brenda, Corinne, Craig, Diane, Dubya Jay, E., Gina, Greg, Kevin, Loretha, Tricia, Vaness, Virgil. And my family . . . sorry, too many of y'all to mention . . . THANK YOU for your support! A special thank-you to my BFF and confidant for over forty years, Leslie Gates; you rock! And to Keith and Mary Kay Carodine for being awesome parents to our amazing sons, Miguel and Clay; you are blessed and loved — breath, blood, and bone, I cherish the light and legacy that you are in my life.For my Best Buy guy, Kerwin Matthews . . . thank you for letting me share part of my journey with you. And for my Mommy and Daddy, Geraldine and John Spencer, I am ever so grateful for your love, patience, and acceptance of this curious, courageous, and creative wild child, and for making me a woman of strength and character.

Finally, I am forever grateful to YOU, thank you for taking the time to read my story. May you BE a Change Agent. "We are the ones we've been waiting for," and may you always and forever Live 4 Love! Amen.

B.A.G.H.D.A.D.
Yoga

AUTHOR'S NOTE

The words in *italics* throughout my memoir are *Sanskrit*, an ancient language of India. Please reference the glossary in the rear of the book as needed.

THE FLOW!

I am disciplined, physically and mentally tough, trained and proficient in my warrior tasks and drills. I always maintain my arms, my equipment, and myself.
Soldier's Creed

B.A.G.H.D.A.D. Yoga is not completely based on a specific location or entirely about the philosophy of yoga. It is, however, about my personal journey which is based on spiritual principles and mind-body practices that I live by and applied while I served with the United States Army in Baghdad, Iraq, at the Multi-National Security Transition Command–Iraq and taught yoga classes after duty hours during a nearly yearlong deployment that began in June 2006 and ended in May 2007.

During that year I had a shift in consciousness — from breath-holding fear to heart-opening love, and then from an external war to internal peace.

I fashioned the seven letters of B.A.G.H.D.A.D. into the ideals of interconnected spiritual principles, morals, values, and ethics. *Yoga* means to "yoke" or "unify" the mind, body, and spirit. Together the elements of *B.A.G.H.D.A.D. Yoga* represents an evolutionary process of becoming aware and discovering my Soul's purpose with the omniscient Divine connection that we all share.

B

The acronym B.A.G.H.D.A.D. is my definition that describes not an actual place but the Beginning of love: the Birth of my being — to Be. Love is the genesis. Love is who I Believe we all are. We are also the very essence and attributes of opposing forces: light and dark, positive and negative, yin and yang, male and female. These attributes call us to Balance and to practice equanimity so the powerful truth of love is heard. B.A.G.H.D.A.D. is the place where I began my hero's journey. It is where I Believe . . . and have faith in the unseen and trust and know that Being in this present moment is a gift, a Blessing, so just BREeeeATHE!

A

An Agent of change is what Gandhi so emphatically wished that we would be in the world. He wanted us to Act, to do what we can; teach yoga, volunteer, donate, smile, dance, say *thank you* and *please*, recycle — serve honorably. That change can also be a simple shift in Attitude, to see the AWE, the sacred beauty we All share. I call it the "AWE-mazing," "the AWE-some." Or it can very well be the "AWE-ful." Either "AWE"; we always have a choice. And then, we "AUM" — "Ommmm" is the vibrational sound of the Universe, the sound of God, the Alpha and the Ommmmmega!

G

Growing towards God from a conscious awareness calls us to use Grace when we are in fear: FEAR or False Evidence Appearing Real. FAITH trumps fear any given day. We must always Give thanks and Gratitude for the Goodness that God IS all the time.

H

Healing our Hearts is the only way our planet stands a chance. We must act compassionately towards each other, as well as with our environment. We must live Harmoniously and practice Humility. It is the Heaven and/or the Hell that we choose every day. Choose Happy!

D

Dreams shape our journey, and they lead us to open our heart. We must have the Discipline to Deepen our faith and our love, and live an inspired purposeful life with Dignity.

A

Awakening to the infinite possibilities of our Divinity — the AWE-mazing gift we all possess: Our Authenticity.

It means taking personal Action to become Aware of your Soul's purpose. Acceptance of being of service to others and becoming a sacred Activist creating a world that works for everyone.

D

Death of the E.G.O. — Dissolve it. Let the ego go. That little word can be BIG on selfishness and self-righteousness, breeding fear. It is Determined to Destroy our Divinity and our conscience, and undermine our consciousness by trying to Edge God Out of our lives. Just know that a constant Devotion to the omnipotent, transcendent power truly is a Destiny Date with the Divine. Prayer and faith obliterates the ego. The enD, bah bye!

Everything, every experience in between the B of B.A.G.H.D.A.D. and the D, the birth and the death — between the love, the fear, the war, and the peace — was and still is my divine evolutionary process. I am shifting to be a graceful and grateful Soldier: a SOUL-dier, a Warrior, and a Yogini on a sacred heroine's journey.

The tapestry of mystical metaphors, yoga postures, New Age concepts and coincidences, Army jargon and mixed-up "I don't know where I got that shit from" philosophy that I have woven into my memoir reflect my rich cumulative life experience thus far; a life journey that has been full of symbols, spiritual insights, historical events, epiphanies, and Soulful healings. I am neither expert nor master in any of these concepts, mind you, but an active spiritual seeker, a connoisseur for my own self-discovery so I may do the work to be a better human.

I tell my story using my personal dramas that have unfolded everywhere from my humble beginnings in my hometown of Bakersfield, California, to the heated battles in Baghdad, Iraq, and beyond.

On my journey I encountered numerology, the cosmic study of numbers. The number seven is a spiritual number. It is the number that appears most frequently in religious texts. For example, in the King James Bible, Matthew 18:22, Jesus says, in advising his disciples on how many times to pray for forgiveness, "I say not unto thee, until seven times, but, until seventy times seven." Jesus says pray without ceasing . . . all seven days of the week on all seven continents. Bestselling authors Stephen Covey and Deepak Chopra told the world that there are *7 Habits of Highly Effective People* and *Seven Spiritual Laws of Success*. And I bet if you went to Las Vegas this very second and watched a gambler playing on the slot machines, he'd be happy to hit Lady Luck 7–7–7. Serendipitously, Baghdad has seven letters, so consequently *B.A.G.H.D.A.D. Yoga* has seven chapters that will shift and flow as a salute to the sun.

The sun of course is the star that lights our day, warms us, and revolves for our growth; consequently, the Sun Salute (*Surya Namaskar*) is a yoga sequence that is the foundation for many yoga styles that energize and evolve us. This graceful sequence is a series of flowing physical movements of linked yoga postures (*asanas*) that are designed to warm up the entire body, building strength, increasing flexibility, and establishing the integration of body, mind, and spirit. At the beginning of each chapter I will introduce you to one of the seven basic *asanas*: Mountain Pose (*Tadasana*), the Forward Bend (*Uttanasana*), the Low Push-Up (*Chaturanga Dandasana*), the Cobra (*Bhujangasana*), the Upward-Facing Dog (*Urdhva Mukha Svanasana*), the Downward-Facing Dog (*Adho Muka Svanasana*), the Warrior I (*Virabhadrasana I*), and the Lotus Pose (*Padmasana*).

The spiritual guidelines of the eightfold path, known as the eight limbs of yoga or *Ashtanga*, will also be defined in each chapter as translated from the wise sage Patanjali, who has been referred to as the "Father of Yoga." Patanjali roamed India somewhere between 200 B.C. and A.D. 200. His spiritual guidelines serve as a method of discipline for yogis as they aspire to spiritual enlightenment through the practice of yoga.

Numbers, like colors, are cosmic "signs" that are all around us every day, beckoning us to be present, listen, be still, and become a witness; an inside and outside observer. Like the seven colors of the rainbow after a rainshower, the sign or message is God's promise that the earth will not be flooded again. These beautiful colors signal that the storm has passed and clear skies are ahead. The rainbow's spectrum of colored light that sparkles and shines through the water particles is the same pattern that flows through our bodies.

The seven chakras are symbolic rainbow particles that shine in and radiate through our bodies. These energy centers are represented as colored wheels of light that are invisible to the naked eye, but they can be felt and sensed intuitively. I highlight the chakras with the hope that you will discover the correlation between how these colors and their location in your body affect how you live. Maybe you will see how they affect the way you internalize and synthesize information, and the way you respond to a myriad of stimuli.

I would be remiss if I did not include the Army's seven core values of Loyalty, Duty, Respect, Selfless Service, Honor, Integrity, and Personal Courage; the first letters of each of these values spell the acronym LDRSHIP. These Army values begin each chapter. Leadership is the fundamental process of motivating others to discover their personal power, being accountable, taking action, and accomplishing the goal and mission with cohesive teamwork.

I believe being a leader is something we all must do. Some people may lead military battalions or companies, while others may lead a PTA meeting, a charity to benefit survivors, or a blood drive, or even lead an epic historic event like the March on Washington. There are literally hundreds of thousands of books on leadership styles, philosophies, and techniques. But to me, I believe the key ingredient to becoming a great leader is to live as an inspiring example for others to shine in their own life.

Finally, a succinct definition of the seven principles of Kwanzaa ends every chapter. Dr. Maulana Karenga created the seven principles, or the *Nguzo Saba* in Swahili, in 1966 as the first African American holiday.

The seven days of a Kwanzaa celebration take place

in December and reinforces the basic values of African culture, which stress the importance of building family, community, and culture. I also believe these principles celebrate our global community and reaffirm the bonds between all people that strengthen our world. And for that dynamic affirmation, I say *ashe*, amen, so it is!

B.A.G.H.D.A.D. Yoga is not a close-combat story. Needless to say, I don't divulge any Army secrets, nor did I break down doors, climb through windows, scream profanities, or draw any loaded weapons. I never ever carried an injured buddy to safety after a long, drawn-out firefight with the enemy under the cloak of darkness, or saw bloody body parts flying in the air after a catastrophic blast. The heat of my battle wasn't with Sunni or Shiite Muslims, Al-Qaeda, or some multisyllable unnamed enemy. Yes, mortar fire was often too close for comfort, and I was in harm's way each day of my deployment. But my enemy was anxiety, arrogance, apathy, ignorance, stress, and the petty, toxic people I met who kept me in fear for my life, challenging my values and my integrity. I fought for my peace of mind. I duked it out with depression and kept hope alive and survived the dark nights of my Soul with yoga, mind-body practices, spiritual acumen, and my family covenant.

I share my story, my experiences, my truth so it can be a catalyst for positive change for others — in the military or not. You see, a combat zone is a noun . . . it can be a person, place, or thing. It can be anywhere a person does not feel safe and secure . . . rooted. A place where they may feel threatened or invalidated. It is a dangerous zone. You don't have to be in Baghdad, 6,000 miles away; you can be at home as a victim of violent domestic abuse or at work in a environment that is hostile because of your race, religion, age, or gender. Perhaps your combat zone is with your dear friend, or is that friend really your passive-aggressive foe who gets on your last nerve? You can be at war with your finances, your weight, or a life-threatening illness. Whatever YOUR combat zone, even those self-imposed ones . . . I share with you a taste of freedom with *B.A.G.H.D.A.D. Yoga* by encouraging you to shift your consciousness from fear to love, and from war to peace.

If I write vaguely about the facts of my experiences, allow your imagination to fill in the spaces. But please err on the side of the good fight! I still serve my country honorably and will always do so even when I retire from the military. Some names have been changed, and the juicy details you may desire are not chronicled here. In the BIGGER scheme of things, *B.A.G.H.D.A.D. Yoga* is ALL about US collectively changing and transforming to be better citizens and humans. It is about us choosing health, healing, and love over fear, dis-ease.

Although the Sun Salute and the chakra ascension are presented in a progressive sequence, my story is not chronological. Now be forewarned, I often share musings that have absolutely nothing to do with my deployment yet everything to do with the interconnectedness of the "stuff" of US!

When I deployed wearing the cloth of our nation, my intention was to be an instrument of peace, love, and light. The language of the Soul often has no words that can actually describe or explain Its presence. I ask you to read with your eyes, but listen to the cadence of the words, the beat of your heart; allow yourself to drift to the space where we all interconnect. As Baron Baptiste, one of my awe-some yoga instructors has quipped, "We will either be cellmates or SOUL-mates on our planet!" In other words, we can choose to be locked down, disempowered, and kept hostage in a five-by-five cell by ourselves, or be free, open SOUL-diers. I choose the latter. My hope is that one day we may all choose truth and freedom and living for love. Loving is always a choice!

Finally I applaud the senior military leaders, many of whom are medical professionals, and Department of Defense civilians who are committed to the health of our force. Thank you for dealing with what I will call the BIG pink elephant with the purple tutu in the room, which is posttraumatic stress, suicide prevention, care of wounded Soldiers, prevention of sexual assault, evaluation of disabilities, and aggressively taking care of US. Our mental and physical health is central to the readiness of our Army. We are our nation's precious assets!

I pray *B.A.G.H.D.A.D. Yoga* offers you the gift of realizing that we are AWE-mazing works in progress. And that we are spiritual beings in the midst of a human experience that can change our thinking and change our lives with just a shift, to something better, healthier for the common good. I believe militaries, though necessary, don't actually ever win in wars. What wins is the power of people like you and me who strive to lead peaceful lives and set the example for how not to lose one's Soul in the battle. General Douglas MacArthur said it best: "The Soldier, above all other people, prays for peace, for he must suffer and bear the deepest wounds and scars of war."

Please visit the list of resources in the back of the book for your attention, awareness, and activism on how YOU being so AWESOME can be the change!

The Divine in me bows and salutes
to the Divine in you.

B

BIRTH, Beginning, BE-lieve, BLESSINGS, Balance, BREATHE

Mountain Pose (*Tadasana*) or Standing at Attention (*Samasthiti*)

First or Root Chakra (*Muladhara*)

Location	Coccyx or base of the spine to the genitalia
Color	Red or black
Element	Earth
Sense	Smell
Sound	Do
Functions	Action; gives vitality to the physical body, life force, survival, self-preservation, instincts
Glands or organs	Adrenals, kidneys, spinal column, legs, bones
Qualities & lessons	Mastery of the body, grounding, individuality, stability, security, health, courage, patience
Negative qualities	Self-centeredness, insecurity, violence, greed, anger
Gemstones	Ruby, black onyx, hematite, smoky quartz, red jasper, carnelian, garnet

Ashtanga Path

Yamas (Universal morality) — non-violence, non-lying, non-covetousness, non-sensuality, and non-possessiveness

Army Core Value
Loyalty

BIRTH, BEGINNING, BE-LIEVE, BLESSINGS, BALANCE, BREATHE

Breathe. Let go. And remind yourself that this very moment is the only one you know you have for sure.
Oprah Winfrey

All life begins with the breath. Our life force is the integration of *Prana,* which is breath or our vital energy, and *ayama,* which means control. *Pranayama* is a breath control exercise used to attain higher states of awareness. With the life force rhythms of pranic energy I began each yoga class in Baghdad with an intention that I would create an atmosphere of peace and balance, and remind students of their truest authentic potential — the potentiality of being "powerful beyond measure," as prolific spiritual author Marianne Williamson says in *Return to Love.*

Returning to the power of love is what we all must remember. We also must be mindful of our Soul purpose, what we came here on earth to do, to be. We are all born with this great magnificent gift inside us, this life force present to share with others. It is our birthright; ours alone, we own it. I always prayed in the classes I taught that if we had forgotten our Soul purpose or even thought we had misplaced the gift, no worries, it could be found, even in Baghdad. I knew that "There is no fear in love, but perfect love casts out fear" (1 John 4:18) and that everyone has their perfect purpose and passion, and yes, some may even have poison. Yet my prayer and meditation would silently ask the students, "Can you today, this very moment, in this breath decide what you believe and know for sure? Can you live for love? Can you act 'as if' so the universe will conspire to fulfill this truth, your purpose? Be purpose-driven and continue to shift in the highest gear; you are divinely guided and supported. All together now, breathe deep and honor the gift — the present."

I would then begin the class, leading my motley crew of fellow service members to move into their first yoga posture (*asana*), the Child's Pose (*Balasana*). My yoga students represented all military branches of the United States: Army, Air Force, Navy, and Marines. I also had a smattering of students from the multi-coalition military forces from Australia, England, and Italy, and from the Department of State, the FBI, USAID, the United Nations, and defense contractors such as Kellogg, Brown & Root and the infamous Blackwater Security Corporation. No matter the uniform or what our jobs were, the crew's mission in class was clear . . . to unfold, stretch, and breathe together in search of balance.

We all needed to get away and release the debilitating energy of war. Being an unencumbered child in the Child's Pose was a great way to begin our yoga practice. It offered the freedom to relax from our necks to our hips.

"Inhale, Child's Pose, please," I would say. "Now relax your hips to meet your heels. Surrender and open your heart and begin to breathe deep. Extend your arms outward, relaxing your shoulders as you lightly place your forehead on the mat, stimulating the third eye center, the *shiva netra*, or eye of shiva, the seat of spiritual intuition.

"Move your knees to the outer edges of your mat, bringing your big toes together to touch, if you can," I continued. "Inhaling deeply, fill your lungs and fully exhale out of your nose with your *ujayi* breath, your victorious breath.

"Let us be victorious in how we conduct ourselves. Let go of tension, stress, and any worries that we may be carrying right now. Surrender. Release anything that is not of light and that no longer serves you — be powerful, blessed. Now exhale . . ."

After my regular military duty day, I taught yoga three times a week at the Liberty Pool, a Morale, Welfare, and Recreation center in the International Green Zone of Baghdad. The center was a sprawling rest and relaxation retreat area for the troops. Latin salsa night was held on Thursday, and various weekdays featured kickboxing, spinning, and Brazilian Jiu-Jitsu. But Monday, Wednesday, and Friday at 6:00 p.m. was B.A.G.H.D.A.D. Yoga time.

The Liberty Pool was once known as the "playground"

of Saddam Hussein's son Uday. The lore was that he was psychotic. He was rumored to have tortured athletes from the Iraqi soccer team and kidnapped and raped women on the immaculate landscaped property. Despite that ugliness, the white modern two-story building with a rooftop deck was beautiful and provided the yoga class with its very own American playground.

The center housed three different-sized swimming pools: a wading pool with a slide, a deep diving pool, and an Olympic regulation lap pool. The pools were connected under triangular canvas awnings for perfect shading. The space offered plenty of lounging areas and a section for ping-pong and foosball tables. A large flat-screen TV mounted over a fireplace, which always blasted CNN, was in a comfortable reception area with cushy lounge seating.

I began teaching yoga classes after being in-country for about three weeks and getting approval from my superior officer, an Air Force medical service colonel who knew the intrinsic value of yoga and championed my outreach efforts.

On some evenings, instead of Child's Pose, I moved the class straight to the Downward-Facing Dog posture (*Adho Muka Svanasana*). They knew then I was going to work them like a "dawg." Life is about balance, and so is yoga. Sometimes you are goofy like a child — happy, curious, and fearless. And at other times you go at it like a dog, determined with a one-track mind, ferocious and focused. A yoga practice is also gentle, introspective, and restorative. However you begin, with whatever yoga style you practice — be it hatha and all its derivatives: vinyasa, ashtanga, bikram, anusara, iyengar, kundalini, to name a few — the process of yoga, and its flow, will always give you the perfect sustenance when needed. Whether you're standing, twisting, sitting, lying down, inverting, lifting, or reaching, all the movements result in satisfying satiety and equanimity. Balance. Movement balances your mood because during movement our body produces more endorphins, that feel-good "I'm on top of the world" hormone, while reducing the "it sucks to be me—road rage—eat an entire carton of ice cream" stress hormones such as cortisol. Balance is good!

The deep postures and flowing breath that I taught reflect vinyasa, which literally means "linking breath with movement." This movement would take our minds away from the haunting horrors of combat to a place that grounded us to our core. In every class, we released and surrendered and carried away what toxic energy we could through our vinyasa yoga practice.

Whatever the posture, be it Child's Pose or Downward-Facing Dog, it was time to bring it on, to dig deeper, and to let go of all the tension and any thought process that appeared to be limiting our potential from being positively powerful beyond measure. We had to let go of the daily fear we tried to mask. Child's Pose was our humble home base, our true North Star, our compass to direct our practice and to ground us. It was also a place to rest and set aside the noise of combat. In Child's Pose, we literally took the load off by sinking and opening our hips and lengthening our spines and dropping the chatter in our minds. This posture welcomed us to our very own R&R retreat that we could move into a hundred times if we wished. Releasing the load offered some welcome relief to our lower backs. It was no surprise that the twenty-plus pounds of body armor that many of us wore each day to be safe tightened and weakened our muscles, which left us vulnerable to injuries and emotionally fragile.

Case in point, I injured my rotator cuff from the constant wear and tear of taking that hunk of fiberglass protection on and off every day. Upon my return from deployment, I had surgical repair, which later developed into frozen shoulder syndrome. I now have a permanent loss of range of motion and daily low-grade pain. I just thank God I have yoga to keep me thawed out.

The students that attended my yoga classes didn't have individual yoga mats, so they improvised by placing several towels down on the floor to form a "mat" and define their personal space. Beside their mats were their weapons, possibly a M4 rifle and/or a 9mm handgun, and an array of body armor. Our mats and our guns were our weapons and our protection from what ailed us daily. I knew that my yoga classes became the space of home, our home away from home. It was where we found our peace, balance, and calm — the acceptance of what IS.

The truth is, we were off-kilter. Unbalanced. Out of touch in Baghdad. Things were awry. Our chakras, the seven major ones that I refer to throughout this book, are energy centers that are positioned along the spinal column; they form a network through which the mind, body, and spirit act as one. It is a holistic system: a *whole-in-one* system. When a chakra is blocked, or not functioning properly, this unbalanced energy flow can affect us on many levels and can lead to undue stress and illness.

Our first chakra, or the root chakra, is a stabilizing energy force that keeps us grounded. When balanced, it is associated with a healthy desire for the basics in life: food, warmth, and shelter . . . *home*. Like Abraham Maslow's hierarchy of human needs, this self-actualizing theory says if the basic needs are not met, an individual cannot concentrate on the next level in the hierarchy. The need for structure, order, security, and predictability is the root. When this chakra is imbalanced, we may be afraid of life, withdraw from physical reality, feel victimized, operate in a highly selfish mode, or be prone to violence.

So there it is in a nutshell. It is simple (somewhat). War and evil lie at the base of humanity's unbalanced root chakra. But what can we do? We can OMmmm!

All of Life vibrates in harmonic proportions. OM is the Harmony that weaves the tapestry of interdependent relationships, the dance of energy, the dynamic breathing in and out of the infinite consciousness. OM is the music of the universe. OM is the essence of Being restoring peace, harmony, laughter and love.

Deepak Chopra

I have read that the Om/AUM is in every breath, a sacred sound. The AUM, the hum, is considered the all-connecting sound of the universe. This one word, interpreted as having three sounds, represents creation, preservation and destruction.

B. K. S. Iyengar, master yoga teacher and author of *Light on Yoga*, noted that there are various meanings of AUM. "The letter A symbolizes the conscious or waking state, the letter U the dream state, and the letter M the dreamless sleep state of the mind and spirit," he wrote. The entire symbol stands for the "realization of man's divinity within himself."

AUM became the sacred hum of the Tibetans, the *amin* of the Moslems, and *amen* of the Egyptians, Greeks, Romans, and Christians. *Amen* in Hebrew means "sure, faithful" — and the church says, "Amen — so be it!" According to the ancient Hindu teachings of the Mandukya Upanishad, "Om is the one eternal syllable of which all that exists is but the development. The past, the present, and the future are all included in this one sound, and all that exists beyond the three forms of time is also implied in it."

Even the design of this sacred symbol is chock full of mysticism. Visually, OM is represented by a stylized pictograph. A deeper insight into this mystic symbol reveals that it is composed of three syllables combined into one, not like a physical mixture but more like a chemical combination. Indeed in Sanskrit the vowel o is constitutionally a diphthong compound of $a + u$: hence OM is representatively written as AUM.

From the Army to the AUMy — the Yogini in the AUMy; this play on words and its symbolism inspires me. David Swenson, the amazing and humorous ashtanga master yogi, dubbed me "Major Yoga" when I attended his weeklong teaching intensive program at the Asheville Yoga Center in North Carolina in 2004. It was my first yoga-teaching workshop and my military rank was, of course, major.

David will tell you, "Yoga isn't easy." That it is not just about the asana practice, moving gracefully or ungracefully from one posture to the next as in a Sun Salute. For the ashtangi, yoga has eight branches or

The symbol of AUM consists of three curves (curves 1, 2, and 3), one semi-circle (curve 4), and a dot. The large lower curve 1 symbolizes the waking state, the most common state of the human consciousness. The upper curve 2 denotes the state of deep sleep or the unconscious. The middle curve 3, which lies between the waking state and the deep sleep state) signifies the dream state. The dot signifies the fourth state of consciousness; in this state the consciousness looks neither outwards nor inwards. Indian mystic thought believes these states of an individual's consciousness represent the entire physical phenomenon. It signifies the coming to rest of all differentiated, relative existence this utterly quiet, peaceful and blissful state is the ultimate aim of all spiritual activity.

limbs that may even further challenge a person. The eight-fold path requires yoginis to look at their social behavior (*yama*), their inner discipline, and how they treat others (*niyama*). Yoga has its postures (asanas) to allow you to focus on your life force and your breath (*prana*) to purify you. The postures and controlled focused breathing prepares you to withdraw your senses (*pratyahara*) and concentrate (*dharana*) to still the mind and meditate (*dhyana*) towards the ultimate goal of absolute bliss (*samadhi*). Now that is MAJOR YOGA! The eight limbs work together, which builds the foundation for a spiritual life in such an amazingly major way. But yoga is not easy, and as David Swenson says, "you are still a good person" if you wobble, fall out of a pose, or can't even do it physically. What matters is the emotional, mental practice and the intention of evolving, processing, and adapting the eight limbs as a lifestyle to be a better person. As K. Pattabhi Jois has said, "Practice, practice, practice, and all is coming."

"When you pray, you move your feet" is an African proverb that means when you practice honoring yourself and others, you truly move with grace, you hum to a vibration that moves your Soul. Yoga in essence is a body prayer. It hears and answers viscerally and faithfully. Its qualities revive the Soul. It is rejuvenating and redemptive. Yoga heals.

I did not know about the healing qualities of yoga when I first enlisted in the United States Army in 1986. The military was contrary to my rhythm. I had always been a person who marched to the beat of a different drummer, yet I found myself being moved by the Army and its rat-a-tat-tat.

Before raising my right hand to enlist, or moving my feet in prayer and doing a Downward-Facing Dog pose, I was filled with *maya* (illusion) like any other young adult.

I began college at seventeen. My first major was health science for a pre-medicine track at San Francisco State University during the fall of 1980. I always had this desire to be a top-notch doctor and skilled scientist curing cancer or discovering the antidote to some dreadful disease. Well, somewhere between failing chemistry 101, loving psychology, squeaking by in statistics, and passing Chinese herbology and undergoing ridiculous emotional teenage heartbreaks, I thoroughly confused and frustrated myself about my future professional occupation and personal direction. To add to the confusion, I was working as an underage cocktail waitress in a popular hotel bar that was frequented by San Francisco's finest professional athletes and businessmen. It was the "party all the time" pop and punk culture of the 1980s, and I was definitely off-balance. What to do?

Grace happened when I took a course in holistic health and an afternoon hatha yoga class. These courses led me to suspend my traditional college education to attend the Acupressure Institute in Berkeley and complete a certification program as an acupressure massage technician. The complementary and alternative body-mind medicine, Eastern philosophy, and New

Age ideas that I was introduced to seemed to provide answers to my confusion about life — its cycles, health and healing, and relationships — but most of all it provided me an insight into the omniscience of God/Creator/the Universe.

These answers were profoundly intriguing and mystical, unlike Western medicine and that good ole-fashioned religion. My spiritual quest began with a reading campaign of self-help book titles such as *The Web That Has No Weaver* by Ted J. Kaptchuk, *The Road Less Traveled* by M. Scott Peck, *I'm OK—You're OK* by Thomas Harris, *Your Erroneous Zones* by Wayne W. Dyer, *Living, Loving and Learning* by Leo F. Buscaglia, *The Book* by Alan Watts, and *The Celestine Prophecy* by James Redfield. These spiritual and psychological works spoke to me loud and clear. Now books by Deepak Chopra, Gary Zukav, Marianne Williamson, Eckhart Tolle, Ken Wilber, Yogananda, and others in addition to my daily spiritual readings from *Science of Mind* are my go-to inspirational texts.

With the readings, I became a truth seeker, a self-professed mystic. Back then I can say I was a peace-loving California liberal, or some might say a tree-huggin' hippie . . . yeah, sticks and stones! Actually, I was just cool and funky! Couple that lifestyle and attitude with punk-era fashion, a geometric hairstyle with the sides shaven, gaudy beaded necklaces, oversized dangly earrings, and bright-colored lipstick, and I was surely a sight to see — at least to myself. I had absolutely no issues with creative expression, as songs from that era such as "Like a Virgin," courtesy of Madonna, and "Controversy," by my man Prince, encouraged me to dance as if my hair were on fire!

My inFANtuation with anything about the musician Prince inspired me then as much as today to be FREE. "Peace and be wild," he would call out at concerts. I would scream in response with Prince's signature sound, "Owwwwoooowaahhhh!" I moved and grooved to being "out of the box." I obliged myself to be authentic, seeking my truest hum and my own damn drum.

My mother, Geraldine "Geri" Spencer, would always say, "Dare to be different." When I was growing up in a small central California town of Bakersfield, my mother provided the parental license, motivation, and freedom to allow my creativity to grow and bloom. She was my impetus, to use the old Army slogan, to Be All I Can Be and to color outside the lines and act outside of the box!

In my daring youth, aspiring to become a woman of glowing beauty and charm, I entered a couple of beauty pageants, where I showcased my talent of combining modern jazz and urban break dancing with spoken word poetry and rap. After winning the first Miss Black Bakersfield pageant, I was entered as one of California's contestants for the Miss Black America Pageant in 1985. But my over-the-top talent was a bust. I didn't even place. I kept the sash and hung up the tiara!

You see, long before donning before the Army's camouflage, I aspired to be a *Solid Gold* dancer or an MTV video chick wearing sequined hot pants or other inappropriate outfits and extremely long blonde weaved hair. I know — why? Don't judge; I just wanted to dance. I enjoyed dancing and "showing off," as some would call it. Actually it was "showing up" for what I could do and be. I wasn't arrogant or cocky, mind you. I was self-confident, curious, and fearless! Although I didn't place in that national pageant and obviously never became a dancer on *Solid Gold*, MTV, or VH1, for that matter, I learned how to pray, to move my feet and dance to the beat of my own drum. I became so much more, and I learned that the difference between mediocrity and success was commitment. I committed to being better, to always striving for excellence, shooting for the stars, perhaps landing on the moon or a satellite, a very tall building, or some trees . . . Airborne! I promised I would never give up on my aspirations, but strive to be better with great effort, optimism, and true enthusiasm — my greater-yet-to-be!

Perpetual optimism is a force multiplier.

General Colin Powell

I love the axiom, "Lead, follow, or get out of the way." I enjoy being a leader, yet I can definitely be an outstanding, loyal follower just the same. As an artist, I always worked to reveal my creativity and meld it with my Soul's purpose as an activist. I call it being an Art-ivist. Creatively making shit happen: Artist-Activist. Now, the spiritual seeker in me led me down beautiful unknown paths, paths not taken by my closest homies. The road less traveled was my gig all alone.

My life, my story! Grace, charisma, and ingenuity enabled me to move in baby steps with small strides, great lunging leaps, and counterclockwise circles towards my goals and inspirations. I was determined to get somewhere. I paved my own way, as we all must do. I was just a bit quirkier, so to speak. I climbed many arduous mountains, as a true Capricorn goat would. This earth zodiac sign forced me to ascend higher and express inner depths that needed to be unearthed. I knew it was God calling me, revealing Her ever-creative divine spirit through me.

D*o what you love. Know your own bone; gnaw at it, bury it, unearth it, and gnaw it still.*

Henry David Thoreau

Once on top of a rocky peak, I either looked over and realized it was the wrong damn mountain or decided a seemingly better BIGGER mountain needed my attention. I believed I could do almost anything in my early twenties; my naïveté and my youthful exuberant ignorance would prove me wrong. Even with hard work, determination, and strong sturdy hooves, sometimes I wasn't able to ascend to my destination. As most folks know, goats will eat almost anything; shoes, rusty cans, and cardboard. Believe me, I know; many times I have had to eat cardboard shoe sandwiches, humble pie, and bitter crow to fulfill a goal. Yet some goals just don't pan out, and it really is okay. Really! We make mistakes, choose poorly, do dumb shit; nonetheless we survive.

You may walk away with your tail between your legs, but your head is held high as you accept your shortcomings and gaffes as yummy treats to help you grow.

So, here we are, my eager, youthful dreams of being a dancing, rapping beauty queen and novice acupressure massage therapist couldn't keep up with mounting financial obligations. You see, I was sucking; I was in a dead-end romantic relationship and I was desperately seeking a J-O-B. I had an overdue college student loan bill lurking in the mail, my tail was between my legs, and though my head was high I really didn't know what to do.

Serendipity graciously entered my life when I went with my cousin Toni to the Army recruiter's office in San Mateo, California, on a fine spring day in 1986. I went to talk her out of joining the Army but was seduced by the advertisement that I really could Be All I Can Be with a JOB with the Army. There was an extra incentive of the Army's repaying my college loans if I enlisted for four years of active duty and four years reserve service that easily got me to wag my tail and say, "Hey dude, where do I sign?"

Perhaps the reason I entered the military shows my willingness and openness, my adventurousness to seek and dance to my Soul's purpose. There I was, raising my right hand and accepting the enlistment oath to protect and defend my nation on July 29, 1986, in military service, for God, Duty, Honor, and Country.

Now, I have to tell you, I am comforted by this oxymoron . . . this paradox of fighting for peace. The Army lulled me because of sincere art-ivist service and for God, duty, honor, and country. It was as though the Army actually called me to it. I succumbed. I hummed. That demanding hum was my Soul forcing me to commit to the work of helping humanity save itself from peril. I would serve as a brave and courageous Soldier acting with compassion and seeking justice for all. What I discovered by taking action, even if it wasn't as clever or successful as I intended, was that if I acted with the intention to make a positive impact on the lives of others, I could not lose. My personal agreement was that I would walk this earth at this moment in time to act selflessly. My prayer as I move my dancing feet is that I die serving my country while trying to make it better for all!

Everybody can be great . . . because anybody can serve. You don't have to have a college degree to serve. You don't have to make your subject and verb agree to serve. You only need a heart full of grace. A soul generated by love.
Martin Luther King Jr.

When it was time for Toni and me to ship off for Army Basic Training, some recruiter SNAFU (Situation Normal, All Fucked Up) sent Private First Class Toni Hadnott to Fort Jackson, South Carolina, and Private First Class Michele Spencer to Fort McClellan in the Deep South of Anniston, Alabama. We were pissed . . . but you know the deal, we drove on.

Fort McClellan was the first permanent home of the

U.S. Women's Army Corps Center, which was founded on September 25, 1952. The base officially closed in May 1999. It was there in 'Bama that I sang my favorite Army cadence at the top of my lungs, marching in my new black spit-shined leather combat boots:

> Mama, Mama, can't you see,
> What this army's done for me.
> They took away my faded jeans,
> Now I'm wearing army greens . . .
> Mama, Mama, can't you see,
> What this army's done for me,
> I used to be a beauty queen,
> Now I date my M16. . . .
> Left, right, left, right.

During one long road march in the humid summer heat during Basic Training, the foliage and fauna of the area was so vibrant and radiant, sparkly even, I could feel the spirits of the Soldiers of yesteryear singing — humming the same cadences, marching the same dusty roads. They too were physically and mentally exhausted, beat down by the backlash of the drill sergeants, yet they chose or were drafted to serve our nation gallantly. Some would go on to World War I, World War II, Korea, Vietnam, or other conflicts in the name of protecting and defending their country. These Soldiers were heroes, like my Grandpa H, my dear father John, or my cousins, in whose footsteps I followed. Some of these heroes are still alive, some are dead; we must honor them all. Though I proudly volunteered to serve, I sometimes think who will go now to serve with dignity and honor?

I am concerned that today our military's ranks have fewer honorable warriors. Fear is at an all-time (illusionary) high, so now we have "worriers." The worriers believe that the terrorists and "evildoers" are going to do us in at any moment if we don't get them first, along with their weapons of mass destruction. The military, in its might and amid the shock and awe of war, has at times been known to break the faux pas rule No. 9 made up by a fellow Soldier, which is "Don't do dumb shit!" Don't break rule No. 9. No matter what the political reasons are that militaries exist, history shows us that there have been heroes, hypocrites, warriors, wimps, whiners, wienies, Soldiers, knights, braggarts, brawlers, and bullies for as long as humankind has walked this earth. There have been wars for power, economics, land, oil, crowns, and looooove. There is always choice. The choice for some is to move towards peace and justice by fighting for it violently. For others, in the awakened, you become aware and still and you shift. You shift your consciousness!

Paradigm shifts in consciousness are thoughts about how to do, be, process, and discover more effective ways to achieve a stated goal in a completely different direction. It could be a 180-degree twirl — a beautiful pirouette, a tiny nudge of a shift, or a flap of a butterfly wing. Yet a shift changes things. A change in your mind can be like dominoes standing in a line that fall down swiftly: a chain reaction that can't be halted or steered. The only recourse is to go with it, shift into neutral, relax, and allow the flow. Form following function.

The Army's function provided me some structure for my "out of the boxiness"; it gave me boundaries. When you dare to be different, you need some limits so you can align with your destiny. The Army aligned me with what I wanted to be when I grew up, and to who I am . . . which is strong, Army Strong! Focused. The alignment of what you desire requires an action for manifestation, a laser focus. No successful person arrives there without some kind of carrot-inspired direction and intestinal fortitude.

Even a musical one-hit wonder has enough gumption to lift their voices, acquire the studio time, and somehow, someway mint a track with a hook that stays played on the radio every ten minutes, and we end up humming that tune all day. We might even say, "That's my song, my jam," throw our hands up and wave them like we just don't care! And then . . . the hit grows old, tired, and we move on to the next Top 40 song. The one-hit wonder is played out, yet they sang as we must do over and over, and choose to make hits, to lift our voices and align everyday in the flow to rejoice and hum to the tune of our Soul.

In yoga, we align ourselves on the mat over and over again, and wonder how our bodies respond to the movements. One day your practice flows gracefully, the energy is boundless and you lift, reach, and breathe . . . effortlessly. The very next day, your mat wrestles you, taps you out; you choke, cough, or even shed tears, for every stretch feels like you might rip something deep deep inside so you surrender, accept, shift, and lay still, safely in the aligning comforting arms of *Savasana*, humming the tune to the rise and fall of your chest.

Basic Training shifted me big time at the core level; not only did I surrender my inner *Solid Gold* dancer, but I no longer desired to be an enlisted Soldier a year later. I needed a greater challenge: to finish my bachelor's degree and lead from the front as a military officer. When that inspiration came in from the ether, I went with it and flowed. I changed direction, realigned myself, and sought to earn my presidential commission. The Army program was called Green to Gold. If an enlisted "Green" Soldier had a certain number of college credits, they could transfer from active-duty status to become a full-time student with an accredited college that offered the Reserve Officer Training Corps (ROTC) program. After following my inspired calling, within three years of my initial enlistment I shifted from a private first class to a ROTC cadet with the California State University–Fresno Bulldog Battalion, and finally received my "Gold" as a shiny butter-bar Solid Gold second lieutenant . . . Owwwwooooowaahhhh!

Not to bore you with all the beautiful complexities and consequences of my life shift, but by the time I graduated from college in 1990 as a distinguished military student and was commissioned as a second lieutenant, I had married, had a beautiful baby boy named Miguel, divorced after a year, promptly married a wonderful professional man, and conceived a second son, Clayton. Life's twists, turns, and shifts had offered me two marriages, two children, two divorces, and a partridge in a pear tree by 2001. Several promotions in rank, changes in duty positions and locations, and a wide range of civilian occupations came and went by the time I got the Army's mobilization alert message, Raging Bull, in 2005. The alert was official notification that my Army Reserve unit had been resourced and selected for an Operation Iraqi Freedom deployment.

T*he most important kind of freedom is to be what you really are.*

Jim Morrison

I had just turned forty-three, so the news of the deployment led me to do some introspection and self-analysis of my values and beliefs, and my strengths and weaknesses. The subsequent personal growth had formed lines on my face from smiling, laughing, and crying. The beautiful strands of silver throughout my hair glistened with my coming of age and wisdom. I took an inventory of how I lived my life; it was and forever will be filled with passion, purpose, and integrity. The lessons from my parents, drill sergeants, superior officers, family and friends, and so many others instilled pride, hard work, humility, honor, respect, and determination. I knew I had one life to live, so I prepared to buckle up, stay alert, stay alive, and get ready for the ride. I was on my way to war!

Not so fast, first stop . . . I needed a beach retreat. I needed some yoga, I needed power; I needed a Power Yoga weeklong retreat in Hawaii with renowned Master Yogi Baron Baptiste. Just two months before deploying I discovered more depths to my Soul purpose with Mr. Baptiste's unique way of asking "excavating questions" to the future teachers attending his Level One yoga teacher training. "What lies deep within you?" "What's your story?" "What's behind the mask?" he asked us after marathon yoga practices.

The answers were written in private journals or shared aloud. Whichever way we communicated our new way of being, the process was transformative for each one of us. Yoga can break you down physically, emotionally, and spiritually to enable you to have a breakthrough to a whole new you by peeling away the layers, the masks of deeply ingrained and embedded decaying bullshit! I completed the weeklong retreat feeling renewed, refreshed, and energized, and completely committed to keeping fear at bay. I was deeply inspired and empowered to teach yoga in Baghdad with a Soul power generated by love . . . even though I couldn't pronounce all the postures in Sanskrit or do a cool handstand. I was going to be teaching with Soul!

I must also tell you another source of my yoga teaching aspiration. Sometime in 2003, my friend Peg introduced me to an old church turned yoga studio called The Sanctuary in Gainesville, Florida, and it became my personal refuge and salvation. Though I was introduced to yoga when I studied acupressure massage therapy in 1985 and had followed along with Bryan Kest's *Power Yoga* videos, it was the studio, the ambience, the sense of sacred space and ritual that became the place where I could surrender to the rhythm of my heart and really get my OM on. Having a regular yoga practice at The Sanctuary allowed me to breathe again and emotionally process my divorce after ten years of marriage, a brief rebound-deflating relationship, and a hostile work environment as an Army ROTC associate military science professor at the University of Florida. Yoga heals.

Attending The Sanctuary yoga studio gave me the idea that I could teach yoga because I had been teaching ROTC for the past three years, and I absolutely loved interacting with students, hoping they too would serve honorably. Clearly both philosophies enable, encourage, and inspire students to Be All They Can Be, An Army/AUMy of One, Army/AUMy Strong! The ROTC motto is Leadership Excellence, which expresses the ultimate responsibility in the discharge of our duty to the nation — being excellent and leading from the front. The military profession and yoga is built on service (*seva*). We are military service members. Our Army core values spell LDRSHIP: Loyalty, Duty, Respect, Selfless service, Honor, Integrity, and Personal courage. With such attributes and coveted characteristics, I could not think of being committed to any greater profession — the profession of arms.

I wrapped my arms around teaching and being an agent of change. I would lead from my heart, hoping that whenever I was given the opportunity, I would lead from the strength of humility and compassion, and not from fear and violence.

It is important to note again that a shift in consciousness is when you seek and ask big questions such as "What am I born to do?" "What is my Soul purpose?" "What do I believe?" I believe we don't ask these kinds of questions of ourselves often enough, or delve deep enough because we fear what we may find. And if we discover a part of ourselves that we aren't too fond of, we may actually have to change, and that means taking action; taking a risk to change our behavior, be accountable, be responsible, and stand at attention. The yoga posture *Samasthiti*, which literally translates to "stand at attention," is a posture within the Mountain Pose of *Tadasana*. These yoga postures require a person to be attentive, standing upright, with feet firmly yet lightly on the earth. Grounded.

It is in *Tadasana* that one can lift the body's core to have it move gracefully to the next posture. Arms hang at the sides, eyes at a forward gaze — a *Dristi*, meditative, relaxed, and focused. In the military's position of attention, a Soldier's head and eyes are focused forward, body erect, heels together, legs and arms straight but not locked, chest lifted, and — get this — "silent unless otherwise directed." In yoga also one must get silent; stilling the mind and becoming intimately acquainted with one's core, one's strength, one's *uddiyana bandha* or "upward lifting lock." A *bandha* is an energy lock that anchors and roots your body for stability in a movement. When we are strong in our core we have the opportunity to be our very best

39

because we are operating from the center of who we truly are — which is powerful beyond measure! Being present at attention, being ready, not hurried, for the next movement, living in that moment when the heartbeat and the breath are synchronized perfectly. It is the awareness that life only can be lived from there — in the moment. Not in the past or future, only just then: moment after moment. Instead of clearing your throat, shouting, or raising your hand and announcing your arrival, it is your presence; it is your energy that exudes the life force that is meant to be shared and given unconditionally, bellowing, "I Am Here!"

So that's what I believe. I Am showing up, I AM here, I Am being truly present and accounted for in my life and in the lives of others with grace, in this very moment. I AM paying attention. This belief requires that I take action, so that is why I created B.A.G.H.D.A.D. Yoga: to awaken. For I believed that to be asleep at the wheel of life is dangerous — for REAL!

The yoga posture Wheel or Upward Bow (*Urdhva Dhanurasana*), has an element of danger also. It's a backbend. You begin on your back and your core lifts up and up so only the soles of your feet and palms of your hands are firmly grounded on the floor. Your back arches in a bridge high enough that a tiny man can crawl underneath you, and your back shifts and transforms. When you're performing the Wheel, the chest expands, the shoulders strengthen, and the tension in the hip flexors can release. This asana is not for the weak of heart; it is a transformative movement, which expands and opens and awakens your heart like no other. Yet still, you must be ready to shift, willing to explore your limitations in any posture and throughout your daily living. For Wheel, for REAL, we can no longer sleep or live our collective lives under the bridge, in the shadows, behind the scenes in a cubicle, on the sofa zoned out watching E!, ESPN, BET, CNN, CSI, HGTV, MTV, NBA, NFL, or any other abbreviated show. Wake up! It is show-up time. This is your REALity show! "We are the ones we've been waiting for," as the Hopi elder says.

Before I deployed to Iraq for Operation Iraqi Freedom, I consciously transformed, expanded, and gave my all to pay attention to the details. God is there in the details. My journey to the combat zone shifted to my ride in the freedom zone and a new way of being. My life as a Warrior, Soldier, Soul-dier, mother, sister, daughter, citizen, and even as a novice yoga instructor raised the question "What do I believe?" That question and many other introspective queries flooded my mind as I prepared for my deployment. Fearful at first, I began with some pretty pathetic morbid questions: Would I get killed? Would I have to fire my weapon and kill? What if the perpetrators were children like my sons? I wondered if an explosion would consume me and leave my parents with nothing but a few ashes and old cavitied teeth to bury. How would I stay grounded? Motivated? Confident? Would I remain emotionally agile when conflicts became crippling? Moreover, home was thousands of miles away. Could I cope?

I was a fully trained Army officer with more than twenty years of experience; I believed in a deeper purpose of my role as a warrior, albeit a peaceful warrior, not a worrier! I shifted and answered those dark questions with the Peace Prayer by St. Francis of Assisi:

Lord, make me an instrument of your peace.
Where there is hatred, let me sow love;
Where there is injury, pardon;
Where there is doubt, faith;
Where there is despair, hope;
Where there is darkness, light;
And where there is sadness, joy.

This affirmative prayer was the solid rock that I stood on during the year in a far-off location that would challenge me, inspire me, and ultimately awaken me to discover more of my Soul. At other times, I found solace simply by calling my momma . . . MawwwwMa!

Enough about me; let's get back to my deployment to Iraq. OK, here we go . . . let's sing . . .

Here we go, here we go . . . all the way,
Here we go . . . all the way.
C-130 rollin' down the strip!
Airborne Daddy gonna take a little trip
Mission unspoken, destination unknown,
Don't even know if we're ever coming home!
Army Cadence

"Attention," yelled the chalk leader. The command jolted me from my reverie. He was one of the non-commissioned officers in charge of getting us Soldiers onto the chartered plane that would fly us to our next place of duty and service, Baghdad, Iraq. My focus was not on the myriad of morbid questions I asked myself, but on being balanced to offset my anxiety. Baghdad, I decided, would for me be a place where I would maintain and hold the light. That light would shine, free my Soul, and banish my fear. *Is this a blessing or a curse to be sent off to war?* was the last question I asked myself as I boarded the plane. I chose to answer the question with the affirmative *It's a blessing!*

After getting our attention, about three hundred Soldiers from the 108th Division (Institutional Training), headquartered in Charlotte, North Carolina, were instructed to assemble into a final mass formation for accountability. For the umpteenth time, I presented my dog tags and my identification card. I cleared my magazine-less weapons: an M4 rifle and a 9mm handgun that I would be figuratively married to for the next year. I would have to carry my "beloveds" and my "full battle rattle," which is a body armor vest, a Kevlar helmet, an assortment of attached pouches and pockets that can carry ammunition and the essential necessities such as lip gloss, sunscreen, candy and protein bars, notepad, pens, and tampons . . . MY shit!

My shit seemed to weigh close to a million pounds as we moved around in zillion-degree heat or whatever temperature it is in Hell. All right, so I exaggerate a smidgen, but I was wearing more than twenty pounds of battle rattle in temperatures ranging from 120 to 140 degrees. I had so much ammo in my satchel pocket that my overall body weight increased to that of the infamous fat lady. Transporting all that gear was my very own "fifty million pound" challenge. Oh, how many times I just wanted to sing like that fat lady. "Is it over yet?" Because before we boarded that chartered plane or stepped one foot in Baghdad we spent two months on three weeks' worth of training; in other words we wasted a lot of time on our pre-mobilization training and I was totally over it!

Pre-mob training was conducted at Fort McCoy, Wisconsin, in the middle of nowhere. It involved familiarizing ourselves with the latest military tactics, techniques, and procedures, convoy operations, various weapons systems, the extremely deadly improvised explosive device (IED) technology, hand-to-hand combat (combatives), and the Arabic language and culture.

I was serious about this training and received GOs — passing marks — on all the required tasks ahead of most of my peers. I exemplified strong leadership, mentally and physically. I was determined to stand in the light and not in the shadows of doubt and impatience with bullshit. We had plenty of down time during this crucial training period, so when I asked my senior leaders for a 24-hour travel pass to see my son Miguel graduate as a MVP high school football player from P. K. Yonge Research Development School in Gainesville, Florida, and was denied, I felt the first of many stabs to my heart.

The reason, the leaders explained, was that if they let me go, then other Soldiers would want the same privilege. *Really? What? This is some bullshit!* I shook my head in disappointment and pouted. I couldn't debunk that absurd rationale without the F-bomb flying out my mouth, so I acquiesced and cussed the leadership internally. I digress . . . I was pissed!

I was a single mother at the time. My greatest joy has always been parenting Miguel and Clayton. Watching your child graduate is a reward for having to help with all those late-night school projects, fussing over homework not being turned in because it was buried deep in the backpack, and attending every after-school sports practice and early Saturday morning ball game. This high school graduation brought the realization that one day very soon I would not have to argue over who left the dishes in the sink, or why a bedroom looked like a pigsty, or why piss was all over the toilet seat AGAIN. You see, I needed to witness my wonderful son receive the diploma to adulthood and passage out of my house. And wouldn't you know it, due to some inane training schedule conflict, the day of his graduation I lay on my bunk all day pouting. I truly sang the blues!

I tell that story to illustrate a personal sacrifice I had to experience that fires me up even today! I know, I know, it's not yogic. Let it go, you say . . . forgive already. I have, and I have learned since to do more deep breathing to surrender and keep it moving without cussing! (Sort of.) In 2010, I saw Miguel graduate with a bachelor of arts degree from the University of Florida, where he was on the national champion football team for five years. Now, how about that blessing?

At times it is the emotional luggage that weighs a Soldier down. It is the military's "hurry up and wait" — or "weight" — that can truly bring on a serious pout. Most Soldiers are accustomed to the "wait" cliché, the heaviness, and the missed celebrations, but it doesn't mean they necessarily get used to it or that it is acceptable. Sometimes the military's rules are like some yoga postures that you have difficulty moving your body into. First, you may have the desire to avoid it altogether or cuss once you are into it or bolt right out of it when you feel a bit of resistance, body push-back, and tension. Yet, if you stay with the posture, breathe, and relax the joints, the muscles lengthen, you accept and surrender to a once-challenging pose to welcome the next one in the sequence, which can be just as difficult and restorative but you stay, you wait . . . and you heal.

The flow of yoga is to accept all postures with the same intention of expansion and transformation. Therefore I am a blessed military officer. Sometimes you can't pick your blessings, like you can't pick your family. You can only accept them, surrender, and transform.

I'm a Soldier; I Am a SOUL-dier! I remembered I signed up for this. It was I who signed all gazillion pages of the Army's enlistment contract. And my college loan was repaid, hello? I thought about my blessings while lying on that bunk bed, and decided to let go and accept that a girl's gotta do what a girl's gotta do, leave my family, put the pouting aside, buckle up my shit, go kick some ass or something, and move out, Soldier!

To think that I was going to war and had the right to bear arms, lock and load, scan my sector within my field of fire, and potentially commence to popping a cap in someone's behind was kind of empowering and freaky, especially as a yogini. I could say to the enemy, in my best Italian accent, like Al Pacino in the movie *Scarface*, "Say hello to my little friend . . ." Instead, I'd strike a yoga pose, breathe deep, and pop off my two peace fingers in deuces towards those acting inappropriately — that's rule No. 9. It's a fake rule but all kinds of people break it ALL the time — just don't do dumb shit.

Believe it or not, I even thought I would break rule No. 9 if some Al-Qaeda terrorist dudes approached me. I secretly wondered whether I would stand there befuddled, staring, heart racing, and peeing in my pants, or would I do what I am trained to do? Would I confidently grab my ammo, charge my weapon, skill-fully identify my target, and pull the trigger? Truth is, I am an expert marksman. Although I would be armed in Iraq, I'm not sure how dangerous I would be if overcome by fear.

"Heartless Haji killer" was definitely not a nickname I wanted. I would have preferred to throw up my deuces in peace and ask, "Can we just get along, brah?" I'd even offer the terrorist dudes a bar of soap, deodorant, orange peanut-butter snack crackers, flavored water, and a breath mint. Yep, that would break rule No. 9!

However as a Soldier, a Warrior, I have the sacred trust to protect, support, and defend the Constitution of the United States against all enemies, foreign and domestic. So I would have pulled the trigger like an expert with one of my peace fingers and called it a day! Booo yoww!

In the sacred Hindu scriptures of the Bhagavad Gita, or the Song of God, it is said that Lord Krishna, the Divine One, reveals the Bhagavad Gita to the Warrior Prince Arjuna during an upcoming battle. In this war, he will have to kill enemies, some of whom are his relatives, loved ones, and revered teachers. Krishna deems it is Arjuna's duty to struggle to uphold righteousness without consideration of personal loss, consequence, or reward. "The discharge of one's moral duty," Lord Krishna says, "supersedes all other pursuits, spiritual or material."

It was MY moral duty to give peace a chance and commit to teaching yoga on some level for the duration of my tour. War is chaos, disorder, and destruction; could I and others truly shift and transform to peace? Yes . . . we can! In Chinese philosophy The Tao, or The Way, can be translated as the sacred path to actually live harmoniously on this planet. MY way, my path, or my moral duty was between Iraq and a Hard Place — living what I believe, upholding righteousness, and standing for something so as not to fall for any- or everything would be MY easy sacred rule No. 7, avoiding the dumb shit of No. 9 at all costs. Surviving the hard place in Iraq, or anywhere for that matter, requires one to be grounded in a sacred higher power, whatever Its name; it is a holy communion with yourself, spiritually honoring what IS.

When practicing yoga one must actually find the sturdy ground, the peaceful path through *Tadasana*, the foundation for all of the standing postures. *Tadasana*'s firm stance is the balance, which improves posture, core stability, and confidence. Attention and presence of mind require integrity of the Soul grounding force. Whatever you Believe, BE present, STAND UP, and BE accountable for your actions. It is your moral duty. Live your truth, follow your very own authentic path, and deeply breathe in Love!

Some people mistake being loving for being a sap. Quite the contrary, the most loving people are often the most fierce and the most acutely armed for battle . . . for they care about preserving and protecting poetry, symphonic song, ideas, the elements, creatures, inventions, hopes and dreams, dances and holiness . . . those goodly endeavors that cannot be allowed to perish from this earth, else humanity itself would perish.

Dr. Clarissa Pinkola Estés

Our chartered plane finally left Wisconsin's Volk Field Air National Guard Base on June 9, 2006, and landed in Kuwait after some fourteen hours and a refueling in Germany. In Kuwait, we stayed at Camp Buehring, which was a temporary staging area and training base for thousands of Iraq-bound troops. It was only fifteen miles away from Iraq's border. This desert camp looked like the moon. Everything was muted shades of gray and tan like the sand. I immediately began missing trees, grass, anything green, my kids, and my momma — home. I thought, *This is going to be a long-ass year.*

This place gave a whole new meaning to the phrase "hot as hell." Kuwait's air temperature was so hot that, as one master sergeant explained, "It's like entering the gates of Hell and saying this just ain't HOT enough . . . bring on some more!" It was like being in a dry heat sauna then being broiled in a convection oven along with a blow dryer on the hottest setting circling and swirling over your body; your body baking and bathing in your own funky pool of never-ending hot sweaty beads. The sunlight was so bright that I thought it would fry my eyeballs in their sockets; needless to say, I never went anywhere without my Oakley sunglasses, sunscreen, and chapstick.

We were at Camp Buehring for five days. We were issued additional military gear; more pouches for MY shit, and the newest body armor. The armor I had earlier at Fort McCoy was the traditional woodland green pattern camouflage, but the Army was transitioning to the current digitized Army Combat Uniform pattern, so a change was required. This armor was a tad, and I do mean a tad, lighter but was supposed to be safer and would provide better protection, so I embraced it.

At Camp Buehring there was a trailer park strip housing American fast food restaurants: McDonald's, Taco Bell, Subway, Panda Express, and Pizza Hut. Just looking at the restaurants brought a bit of home to the austere gray-tan place from hell. A bag of Mickey D's

French fries carried me to heaven; those fresh, hot, salty potato strips brought tears to my eyes, they were so good. To think I had ONLY been in Kuwait for less than a week . . . I really knew this was going to be a long-ass year away from home!

We left Camp Buehring in the middle of the fifth night on an Air Force C-130 plane. Under starry blackness we would land at Baghdad International Airport. We were in full battle rattle again as we were harnessed in the belly of the plane with seat belts that strapped over and across our bodies. We were crammed in there like sardines; mounds of personal gear and weapons in between our legs made it impossible to move. There were no bathrooms, so it was good that we had maintained strict discipline of our fluid intake before we took off on the hour or so journey. Most of us had iPods or MP3 players blasting the tunes to distract us from the incredibly loud roar of the aircraft engines and the desire to pee.

The descent into Baghdad was like no ordinary airplane landing. No slow approach to the runway and gradual stop, it felt like a sharp spiraling nosedive to the runway that came to an abrupt screeching halt. I thought the landing was cool, but others were nauseated.

We shuffled from the plane with our gear, loaded a bus that transported us from the tarmac to our next destination for the night, Camp Stryker, a forward operating base (FOB) within the Victory Base Complex. Victory Base was the headquarters for the Multi-National

Force Command, which housed more than 14,000 multinational service members and defense civilians.

An hour before we landed, we learned that a suicide bomber at a checkpoint near Camp Stryker killed two Soldiers. Now, I suddenly felt nauseated, I was thirsty, and I wanted to pee-pee or boo-boo . . . or run and get out of the wild, wild west. I didn't know which. While riding in the bus we began hearing crackling popping noises. Puzzled or just in denial, I asked a fellow Soldier, "What are those sounds?" He replied, "Small arms fire." I thought, *Yeah, that's definitely the sound of someone trying to kill us!* I had to calm myself quickly; I was emotionally spent from the travel, the time zone changes, the heat, and the gear-lugging. I remember sitting back, smiling . . . breathing in my moral duty as an instrument of peace, thinking, *Be steadfast; be still and know* . . . And I said the Lord's Prayer: *God's will be done.*

I mustered my strength as we disembarked from our airport shuttles to find our gear loaded onto a cargo truck. We positioned ourselves in an assembly line and one by one performed the "duffel bag drag," which means lugging hundreds of stuffed duffel bags from the truck to the ground in an orderly fashion so their rightful owners can pick them up. At bare minimum each of us had two duffels and a rucksack. We carried one on our back, one on our front, and everything else in our hands. It was a tough haul, no matter what. We made jokes and laughed to keep from crying, for sure; we were exhausted yet we all worked together, embracing the suck until everyone had their gear and found their designated sleep tent that night.

That first night at Camp Stryker was very emotionally stressful and physically demanding. The darkness was eerie. There were towering T-walls — massive concrete barriers that lined the camp and made the area look like a surreal scene from *The Lord of the Rings*. And the porta-potties were clearly about one hundred yards away from the tent . . . dammit . . . oh Lord help me. I was scared. I had to acknowledge that fear had a grasp on me. Not to fear for my life everyday would take nothing less than the grace of God. When I lay down on my cot that night, I prayed for grace, strength, and understanding, and to always make it to the porta-potty in time. I was forever grateful that we had reached this foreign land safely. I prayed that we would always be able to perform our military missions professionally with integrity and, most importantly, ethically.

Leaving Camp Stryker the next day, we boarded oversized mammoth armored buses called Rhino Runners to convoy us out. One of these babies costs the federal government $250,000 each. Defense contractors drove them and escorted us. They made salaries up to $200,000 or more a year, not bad for a combat bus chauffeur when the average combat Soldier's salary is about $7.50 a day. Go figure! Our government financed the Iraq war to the tune of about $10 million a month, which by the end of 2009 totaled about $600 billion and more than 4,200 casualties. The costs and casualties have not ceased, by the way.

A military convoy provided the protection to our Rhino Runners by positioning tactical vehicles in front and to the rear with machine gunners emerging from their hatches. We rode along a trash-strewn highway called Route Irish. It was known as the most dangerous road in Iraq. I prayed for the luck of the Irish and a pesky leprechaun with a BIG gun to get us to the Green Zone safely. Traveling down Route Irish alone did not put me at ease; there were no cars on the road at all; zero, zip, zilch. Just us.

I quickly peered out the heavily draped windows as we traveled the desolate road and barren landscape. It looked like a highway, drove like a highway, but it felt bitter and cold, even in the heat. It had unforgiving secrets. I knew that terrorists had masterfully concealed IEDs along the roads on overpasses, in dead animals, in road railings, in bicycle frames, and in Coke cans. We learned about this ever-present danger in safety and cultural briefings. I was at a complete loss how to even detect these devices because the roads were so littered. We drove fast and furious to avoid potential hazards. I prayed and clinched my butt cheeks for the five miles from Camp Stryker to Baghdad's Green Zone.

Once our convoy arrived safely in the Green Zone, I wondered just how safe we really were. We were surrounded and caged in by those concrete T-walls that would offer the sides of our FOB some protection, but mortars hurled through the sky could fall from overhead and explode ON people! *I don't want just side protection*, I quietly protested, *I want walls above me;*

a concrete ceiling, a force field or something. I knew this was not going to happen, so instead my standard Army-issued Kevlar helmet and my two tons of fun battle rattle would have to suffice.

Now, I have always been intrigued by synchronistic events infused with serendipity. Life's moments are not just coincidences, they are divine and orderly. I believe signs and symbols are all around us, beckoning and signaling us towards the fulfillment of our highest spiritual good. These symbols, signs, and numbers revealed some very interesting concepts to me during and after my deployment. As I mentioned earlier, I was assigned to the U.S. Army Reserve 108th Division (IT), 9th Brigade. Inspired by numerology, I will share what I discovered:

The Mystical Meaning of 108

The number 108 is an especially significant spiritual number and various traditions ascribe different qualities or meaning to it. In the number sequence 1-0-8, 1 stands for God, or higher Truth; 0 stands for emptiness or completeness in spiritual practice; and 8 stands for infinity or eternity.

The Pentagon: The angle formed by two adjacent lines in a pentagon equals 108 degrees.

Some say there are **108 paths to God.**

Buddhist mala, or prayer beads, consist of a string of 108 beads plus one for the "guru bead," around which the other 108 beads turn like the planets around the sun.

Astrology: There are 12 zodiac signs and 9 planets. 12 × 9 = 108

In **Buddhism**, there are said to be 108 earthly desires, 108 human lies, and 108 human delusions, or forms of ignorance.

Meditation: With only 108 breaths in a day, enlightenment will come.

Also in **Buddhism**, there are said to be 108 feelings, with 36 related to the past, 36 related to the present, and 36 related to the future.

The **Sanskrit alphabet** has 54 letters. Each has a masculine and feminine form, Shiva and Shakti. 54 × 2 = 108

Sun and Earth: The diameter of the sun is approximately 108 times the diameter of the earth. The distance from the sun to the earth is approximately 108 times the diameter of the sun.

Moon and Earth: The average distance of the moon from the earth is approximately 108 times the diameter of the moon.

Chakras: There are a total of 108 energy lines converging to form the fourth chakra, the heart chakra. This energy leads to the crown chakra, the seventh chakra, and is said to be the path to Self-Realization.

And oh by the way, my office room number when I was writing the bulk of this book was 108 . . . Divine Order!

Master yoga teacher Shiva Rea used the number 108 in the Global Mala Project, which she founded in 2007.

Rea is a leading teacher of Prana Vinyasa Flow and Yoga Trance Dance. The purpose of the Global Mala Project is to unite the global yoga community from every continent to form a "mala around the earth" through collective practices based upon the sacred cycle of 108.

September is National Yoga Month, and in the Army September is Suicide Prevention Month. It is a month for healing and change. During the fall equinox, which arrives between the 20th and 23rd of September, people from all walks of life celebrate the changing of the seasons in some way.

In the yoga world, there are specific works to further the proclamation of the United Nation's International Peace Day. Yogini Rea began the Global Mala Project with 108 studios, although now many more participate. Yoginis contribute in this global offering by practicing 108 sun salutations (or variations of 27 and 56); 108 rounds of mantra (chant); and 108 minutes of meditation, kirtan-chant, or movement meditation. The funds raised during this event go directly to community service organizations such as Trees for the Future, YouthAIDS, War Child, (Product)RED, and the Global Fund.

Just imagine the energy that shifts during this event and others that are meant to serve and awaken us to our own humanity and compassion. This type of service goes straight to healing our heart and creating peace. It is our very own rescue mission! The heart of the matter in this Global War On Terrorism IS that it IS the matter of our hearts! Interestingly enough, the 108th Division was relatively safe during the troop surge that occurred from 2006 to 2007, when so many other service members were killed. We all returned home alive, but like countless troops many have or will suffer the "invisible wound" of war: Posttraumatic Stress Disorder.

PTSD is terrorist activity in a Soldier's mind. The pain, trauma, and sheer terror Soldiers experience and sense is held within them. A study by Walter Reed Medical Center estimated that one in five Soldiers suffer from PTSD. In 2010, the Army Surgeon General's Office released the Army Pain Management Task Force's final report initiated by Lieutenant General Eric B. Schoomaker. In it there were recommendations for a comprehensive pain-management strategy that is holistic, multidisciplinary, and multimodal in its approach to treating Soldiers and other patients with acute and chronic pain. The report emphasized the use of integrative and alternative therapeutic modalities such as yoga, acupuncture, meditation, and biofeedback in a patient-centered plan of care. I have to believe the Army and its sister services are employing the people and techniques necessary to control this rising statistic, but it will require nothing less than the entire global village to help reduce these growing effects from a long-ass war and rescue us from peril.

So what do you believe? Do you give birth to your dreams? What are the blessings that you are meant to bestow on this planet? What are you BORN to do? How can you serve? What signs and symbols have you ignored or witnessed? Can you breathe deeper, longer, fuller, and Balance?

W*hen the power of love overcomes the love of power, the world will know peace.*

Jimi Hendrix

Umoja (Swahili for "Unity"): *To strive for and maintain unity in the family, community, nation, and race*

A
Agent of Change, AWESOME, Attitude

Standing Forward Bend (*Uttanasana*)

Second or Sacral Chakra (*Swadhisthana*)

Location	Lower abdomen to navel area
Color	Orange
Element	Water
Sense	Taste
Sound	Re
Functions	Emotion; procreation, assimilation of food, physical vitality, and sexuality
Glands or organs	Genitals, spleen, womb, bladder
Qualities & lessons	Giving and receiving, desire, pleasure, passionate love, movement, health, family, tolerance, surrender
Negative qualities	Overindulgence in food or sex, sexual difficulties, purposelessness, jealousy, envy
Gemstones	Coral, citrine, carnelian, gold topaz, orange agate, and aventurine

Ashtanga Path
Niyamas (Personal observances) — purity, contentment, austerity, study, and surrender to God

Army Core Value
Duty

Two

AGENT OF CHANGE, AWESOME, ATTITUDE

Be the change you wish to see in the world.
Gandhi

An agent of change; a change agent; being the change; change is good . . . are such lively and transformative clichés! From the late Gandhi to the late science fiction author Isaac Asimov, change is AWESOME. Asimov said, "It is change, continuing change, inevitable change, that is the dominant factor in society today. No sensible decision can be made any longer without taking into account not only the world as it is, but the world as it will be."

Choice is what we have always when we work to shift a seemingly AWFUL situation and make it AWESOME!

I decided to be a change agent in Baghdad by sharing the beautiful gift and blessing of the 5,000-year-old philosophy of yoga to anyone who wanted to learn and practice. The history of the ancient city of Baghdad dates back to the eighth century. Ironically, this war-torn city has had several names: "Gift from God," "The Given Garden," and even "The City of Peace."

As an instrument of peace and change agent, I found myself assigned to the Multi-National Security Transition Command—Iraq (MNSTC-I) on FOB Phoenix Base in the International Green Zone located in the heart of Baghdad. The command's mission was to train, equip, and man the Iraqi military force. I worked in the health affairs section. I was the principal advisor and mentor to Colonel Hassan, the training director for the Iraqi surgeon general. He was an anesthesiologist by medical training and profession, and an Iraqi Sunni. The surgeon general himself was a Shia. At the time I arrived in the country, the sectarian violence between the two sects was at an all-time high. Baghdad was averaging about fifty-six attacks per day, with Shiites killing Sunnis and Sunnis killing Shiites. There were insurgents, foreign terrorists, and the everyday, all-day street crime that was out of control — it was called the "killing season" in the media. Pretty scary stuff!

Almost all Iraqi medical professionals are taught English in the country's universities, so Colonel Hassan was able to communicate fluently with the health affairs team. He had a strong, confident disposition. He had seen much within his country, and he wanted to rebuild and restore it to some semblance of normal. I guess he appreciated Americans and our military. Or perhaps he just tolerated us. Maybe he thought we were just a big fat joke he had to endure. I really do not know. But what I did know for sure was that he wanted his family back.

A month or so before I arrived, the colonel had sent his family, a wife pregnant with twins and a young daughter, to live in Egypt, far away from the escalating violence within their neighborhood. He also had been captured and tortured just weeks before I met him. Fortunately, he was released with minor scrapes and a bruised ego, while many other medical professionals were being assassinated.

It has been estimated that from 2003 to 2006, two million Iraqis had fled to the bordering countries of Jordan, Syria, and Saudi Arabia, or to northern Europe. The Netherlands and Sweden now have a robust Iraqi population. Killing the educated and elite Iraqi professionals has always been a tactic of the terrorists to foster chaos, ignorance, and instability in these regions. When I was there, more than 2,000 doctors had been killed and assassinated in Baghdad, with many more in Mosul. Iraq had 34,000 doctors prior to the American invasion, and by the summer of 2007, 18,000 had fled the country.

Since most educated Iraqis are fluent in English, many became invaluable translators. This was a dangerous job because their countrymen considered translators traitors. Some translators wore ski masks or bandanas wrapped around their faces to protect their identity. At least two command translators were killed while I was deployed, and I am so very grateful for their courage and service. Without them, our jobs as non-Arabic-speaking advisors could not have been accomplished successfully.

I was Colonel Hassan's second American military advisor. As a woman, I thought I would encounter some resistance from him. I did not. I respected him and felt humbled to work with him. He would call me his "sista" and kind of roll his head around with a smile when he said it. My agenda was perfectly clear — be safe, do good, and go home! My health affairs counterparts and I were all charged to mentor him and his small staff to train future Iraqi combat medics so they could provide adequate care to their own injured forces and sustain their medical skills. Unfortunately, I have to emphasize "adequate" because their standards of care by a medic pale in comparison to those of an American combat medic. Ensuring that Iraqi medics could "stop the bleeding and start the breathing" was difficult when they might not have the necessary bandages or IV supplies to replenish precious fluids. They were not even allowed to intubate a patient, which is when a tube is inserted through the mouth down into the trachea, serving as an open airway. The Iraqi medics also didn't have the transportation resources to get the wounded to the adequate medical facilities.

Though Iraqi hospitals offer varying degrees of quality of care, the combat support hospitals on the American forward operating bases provided regular medical care for many of the Iraqi forces. The medical rules of eligibility in combat were not to discriminate between Iraqi and coalition forces when working to save a life, limb, or eyesight. Our highly skilled medical professionals are our greatest diplomatic assets during a war. In the emergency rooms of the combat support hospitals, insurgents, terrorists, murderers, civilians, and military heroes all received the same standard of care. All life mattered and was treated humanely despite the battle. When American doctors treated injured Iraqis, the patients were stabilized and sent back to an Iraqi hospital to be with their families. The government and the minister of health could then account for them . . . or not.

Sadly, it was known that sometimes when the injured Iraqi Soldier returned to Baghdad's Medical City, the largest medical complex in Iraq, they were killed for being part of the newly established Iraqi Security Force. At the time I wrote this book, there had been more than one million Iraqi deaths and almost ten thousand Iraqi Soldier deaths in support of Operation Iraqi Freedom. We all have suffered great losses.

One day my health affairs counterpart, "Doc," and I attempted to give Colonel Hassan some good ole-fashioned American medical advice for training the Iraqi medics. He turned to us and said, in absolutely perfect English, "This is MY Army and I know what I want and how to get it done . . . *Inshallah!*" Then he respectfully excused himself from our office and left us looking at each other, speechless, and rightfully so. I thought, *Awesome!* and nodded my head, sucked my teeth, and smiled in agreement! Who were WE in our infallible American wisdom and arrogance to firmly proclaim that OUR way is the best and the ONLY way? I thought it was arrogant to try to force a culture and government to change according to our American values so they can free themselves from their alleged ignorance. Needless to say, the Iraqis have been doing what they do for centuries. I think they pretty well have it down pat.

I did say "Change is good," and also affirmed that we have choices and perceptions. Perception is reality, and the reality is — what? Is the glass half empty or half full? For the record, most days I felt I was in Operation Iraqi Confusion, not Operation Iraqi Freedom. Where was the freedom when some people, both American and Iraqi, acted holier-than-thou and had an attitude of "my way or the highway"? I didn't know what freedom or winning a war looked like or whether it was even possible. All I knew was that death, despair, and destruction was leading the way, and I wanted change within and out. As an agent of change, I promised myself that I would honor and respect the Iraqi people and their land, and fulfill my American military mission with integrity even if it sucked the marrow from my bones.

MNSTC-I was a purple environment, meaning that it comprised joint military forces: Army, Air Force, Navy, and Marines, and a smattering of coalition forces — Australians, British, Fijians, and I think a guy from the Republic of China. My health affairs senior officers were from the Air Force and Navy. There were approximately ten Active and Reserve service members, three Iraqi medical professionals or translators, and Doc. Doc was a civilian contractor and a retired Special Forces medic with more than thirty years of service. He was my mentor, a living legend, and boy did he have connections for getting pharmaceuticals! We ran an unofficial in-house wellness clinic for the run-of-the mill ailments, such as typical cold symptoms and the Baghdad crud that included explosive vomiting and the Hershey squirts. We also discreetly treated a few local nationals and some Iraqi security forces.

Our offices were white double-wide trailers. A narrow hallway split the trailer into two sides. The trailer had about eight offices. I shared my office with Doc, an Air Force physician's assistant, shelves of medical supplies, and ceiling-high stacks of boxes filled with clothing and toys that were earmarked to go to Iraqi orphanages. Our office complex was situated between those eerie T-walls and was surrounded by aging sand bags. A convenient concrete blast bunker was just outside our back door. Phoenix Base was originally an elementary school until we seized it as an operating base. The hardened buildings housed the commanding general and his supporting staff and other MNSTC-I teams.

There was no personal housing on this forward operating base. We either commuted by a shuttle or braved the walk from the U.S. embassy area or from FOB Blackhawk. Phoenix Base was self-contained with an amazing dining facility, a motor pool protected by Fijian guards, and a couple of absolutely gorgeous bomb-sniffing German shepherds. A coffee bar was established in one of the buildings where I had an afternoon espresso and purchased packs of Iraqi cookies, M&M's, and other sundries to stash in one of my many ammo pouches. Our offices were equipped with everything we needed: an air conditioner, computers, phones, water, books, and a place to stack our body armor. We always carried at least one weapon, primarily our 9mm pistols, and stacked our M4 rifles in the office. I kept the pistol on my hip in a holster, though many others wore leg holsters. I wore a leg holster for a few weeks; I thought it looked cool, until I couldn't manage the release system when I went to the bathroom — very awkward, to say the least.

My typical workday started about 7:30 a.m. and consisted of responding to email, going to a meeting of some sort, jaw-jacking with Doc, evaluating the Arabic translation of the combat medic course, checking on mail (everybody loves mail and care packages), preparing for a visit to one of the Iraqi regional training centers, or visiting the surgeon general's office located on another FOB about a block away. My workday lasted till about 6:00 p.m. or later, but on yoga nights, I left at 5:30 to walk the half block in full battle rattle to the Liberty Pool. So pretty much it was *Groundhog Day* for the duration of my deployment . . . same basic day-to-day tasks, a weekly run for the bunker from a mortar attack, but the true highlight of any given day was going to eat at the feeding trough in the dining facility, or DFAC.

Let me tell you about the buffet-style "trough" where I had the guilty pleasure of chowing down daily. I ate everything from chef-carved prime rib, crab legs, and lobster tails to gyros and fresh-mex tacos. A short-order line of hamburgers, grilled cheese, hot wings, and seasoned fries and gargantuan salad bars were available every day and everywhere. You may be thinking, "How extravagant and accommodating to have so much variety." Really? A home-cooked meal at home trumps any all-you-can-eat-surf-and-turf buffet at war!

Vegans were out of luck at the DFAC, and probably most vegetarians had a tough time coordinating their diet. I had changed my diet some years before to eat only fish and soy protein, eliminating beef, pork, and poultry. Seafood was limited, so I was a bit food-challenged as well. At some point around the halfway mark of my deployment, I had a fried crispy chicken tender and I fell in love again with that crunchy, battered succulent meat . . . de-lish! Chicken tenders and seasoned fries became my serious comfort food of choice — that and a blue Gatorade.

It was at the DFAC that we caught up with our comrades. It was like a daily family reunion that we hadn't been to in years. We were just so happy to see a fellow Soldier, even the one with the foul breath and the jacked-up grill. It wasn't like the fake enthusiasm you feel when you see your elderly aunt with the overgrown moustache, who says, "I remember you when you were a baby, how much you've grown . . ." then plants a wet sloppy kiss on your cheek that leaves a lipstick stain that can only be removed with WD-40 . . . yeechk! This was true camaraderie and esprit de corps — enthusiasm!

We were just happy to see all our military family, and especially any new faces.

New faces meant rotation. I could calculate by the newly arrived "fresh meat faces" when my rotation was nearing its end. Tour rotations were ninety days for most physicians. Some airmen and marines had tours of six months or less. The Soldiers from the 108th Division had twelve-month rotations. Others embraced the suck of the surge of 2007 to the newly implemented combat tour of eighteen months — aarrgh!

As we ate our seven-plus-course meals that were carefully selected from the feeding trough buffet, chasing it all down with various colored Gatorades, sodas, or tropical boxed juices, we visited with our adopted Army family, watched CNN on several flat-panel TVs mounted on the DFAC walls, and pretended that all was well. We smiled, hugged, and slapped each other on the back, we celebrated life — we were alive. It was business as usual — just a normal day at war in Baghdad. We loved the DFAC most of all because we were able to forget the outside beasts that were lurking.

A beast is any person, place, or thing that tries to hold you back and deter you from your true self and your purpose in life. Beasts are shadows trying to block your light. Beasts are everywhere. Some are just in your head. A few may be co-workers or even family members, but we all have them. What we do, how we control them or even feed them, is entirely up to us. Being an agent of change takes great courage and commitment. It is the ultimate beast changer.

Major Michaels, the base headquarters commandant, called the command structure "The Beast." Many mornings he talked with me at breakfast about how The Beast was sucking the marrow from his bones. Commandant Major Michaels had a tough, often comical, and thankless job. As commandant, he was like the mayor of a city with no real authority or power because the governor had stripped away his ability to make logical decisions. I observed that Major Michaels did have some important daily tasks, but it was the mundane, grinding tasks, like making sure our vehicles were parked in the motor pool in their assigned spots, or that all the signs on buildings conformed to the latest placard standard, that became petty responsibilities. If one did not strictly adhere to The Beast, it could mean the marrow of your bones would be sucked dry or you would get a simple ass-chewing. So the major ensured that our weapon-clearing barrels were neatly painted, and he responded promptly to our requests for cable and Internet service in our living quarters aka hooches.

The Beast formally scolded me once for bringing my yoga mat into the DFAC and harassed me for my "unruly" hair. I was instructed to keep my thick, coarse hair pulled back in a ponytail because it didn't look like I was meeting Army standards, which said that my hair length had to be above the uniform collar. I assure you it was, but I was tired of feeling my marrow leak from my body and my ass getting chewed by The Beast so I kept my hair neatly brushed and gelled back into a baby bun until my tour ended.

Here you see an example of two senior and field grade officers with more than forty years of combined military service in the middle of a war, thousands of miles away from home, being monitored, reprimanded, and scrutinized over some silly bullshit. It was this type of frustrating, toxic power play that made my tour more hell than dealing with the hell of the war at hand. I felt as though I was walking a tightrope over eggshells and mortar rounds every day.

I lived on FOB Blackhawk. It was across the street from the U.S. embassy, which was Saddam Hussein's former Republican Palace, and it was where the majority of the service members who worked on Phoenix Base lived. FOB Blackhawk skirted the Believers Palace, which was Saddam's massive six-story high concrete and steel bunker fortress. On March 19, 2003, the opening night of the U.S.-led offensive to invade Iraq, our military hurled two 900-kilo bunker-busting bombs at this massive and once beautiful palace. Yet even with that whirlwind of destruction, most of the palace is still structurally sound. It was large enough to house and feed 250 people. It had a large kitchen with its own air filtration system, which enabled it to be fully prepared for an attack with nuclear, biological, or chemical weapons. The palace also had its own generators, which were so powerful they could have supplied the entire Green Zone with electricity. Tunnels were found deep within its bowels that led back to the Republican Palace and to the Tigris River, which was about some two hundred meters away, for a quick getaway. You best believe there were some folks on that fateful day of the attack that ran through those tunnels to get away from those bombs rocking their world. The mighty U.S. military was in the HOUSE and was about to bring it down, singing the ole nightclub refrain about letting the muthafucka burn! And yea, the Army goes rolling along!

I had to look at this twisted, bombed out *muthafucka* structure every day when I went to my hooch-home. It served as a ghostly reminder that I really was not home at all, even though the dusty, swaying palm trees in Iraq were reminiscent of beautiful Florida, California, or some other beachfront property.

My hooch, my ten-by-ten-foot living space, looked like half a railroad car or one of those storage trailer pods. To change the energy I decorated my abode using influences from feng shui, the Chinese art of designing placement. My lavender comforter set, which my family and friends had autographed with inspirational messages prior to my departure, dressed the twin-sized bed. I accessorized it with colorful "happy" pillows . . . so combat chic! I also had a living plant, actually a single ivy cutting, immersed in an empty plastic water bottle that I had cut in half for a vase. It sat on a jagged, charred piece of marble tile I salvaged from the

Believers Palace rubble. All of this was placed on my 32-inch TV set (yes, 32 inches). It wasn't a flat-panel model, so that thing, that albatross, stuck out about two feet from the wall, taking up precious space.

I had some lovely framed family photos and prints of flower bouquets torn from a florist's calendar strategically placed around the room to combat depression and negative energy. Looking at the pictures kept me focused. I knew that what mattered most was my family and getting back to them safely. I had a dorm refrigerator, an essential coffee pot, and an empty box that I decorated with cut-outs of old magazine pictures and favorite quotes. The "pogie bait" snack food box provided me with comforts from home, since I received great care packages from my family and friends. Best of all, in the corner, I had my very own half bathroom with a toilet, a pedestal sink, and a shower. AWESOME!

When I first was assigned to the space, it had bunk beds that were meant to be shared with another Soldier. I was blessed with single occupancy, so I stacked the bunks to conserve space. It was still a tight fit with the two wall lockers, a desk, a nightstand, and that damn oversized TV. Because I typically don't watch much TV anyway and we had very limited access to decent English-speaking channels, the TV really was in my way and taking up valuable space. I eventually acquired a DVD player that was given to me by a contractor who was returning home. Before that I used my 19-inch laptop to watch the latest "haji movies." These bootleg DVDs were sold on the street corners by children or in the vendor markets that we were allowed to patronize. They sold for five dollars or less for two or three movies! Mind you, the sound and video quality may not have been the best for these "still in theaters" movies and they may have had Arabic subtitles, but hey we were in Baghdad! Again . . . AWESOME!

These simple pleasures had a big impact on our quality of life. Watching movies provided lots of joy. I often wondered where those kids and vendors got the DVD copies and those beautifully packaged fake Rolex (NO-lex) watches that sold for ten dollars each. I bought two watches for my sons. Although they only lasted a month or so, they looked like the real thing and my boys thought they were fly as they wore them!

Fast forward from Baghdad in 2006 to Barack Obama's presidential campaign two years later. His platform was one of "hope and change" and "change we can believe in." Obama remarked in his campaign speeches, "I'm asking you to believe. Not just in my ability to bring about real change in Washington, I'm asking you to believe in yours."

Yes we can, we can be agents of change if we believe we have the power to eliminate the beasts. The beasts keep us from the awareness that it is our own attitudes that keep us in the dark cave where they thrive. Our attitudes are our beliefs about the world, and they are reflected on our faces and in the words we speak and the energy we vibrate.

I know that even in war you can be at peace. You can be the change you wish to see in the world. You can be anything you want to be at any time or in any place you desire. You can be in the sweltering heat and have the coolest demeanor. You can be in a fearful place and have the faith that this too shall pass. You can make a choice of power for yourself and others. Your choice can always be either awful or awesome. Your glass can be half full. It will always be my intention to act from a place that increases an awareness of peace for all. You can create and hold a space for others to feel that they too can live from their heart center. And that would be totally incredibly AWESOME!

I will tell you that I'm an empathic person. My heart is open, and so I'm very emotional and sensitive. I cried often in Baghdad, actually boohooing within the private comforts of my hooch. I tried to wrangle my fears and maintain composure when I heard frequent blasts or more often the medical evacuation helicopters that flew all through the night landing at the Ibn Sina Combat Support Hospital within yards of my abode. My hooch would shake, my heart skipping while I held my breath, knowing that another injured fellow Soldier might be fighting for his or her life in the belly of the helicopter.

Emotions like these were always overwhelming, especially after my yoga class. Yoga will make you sensitive to energy because it taps into your inner be-ing, it stretches you and breaks you down during each pose so you can break through to become more alert, agile, and alive. When you practice yoga with positive intentions for change, the practice transforms into a prayer. "It becomes a body prayer," as I heard yogini Seane Corn explain during a Yoga Journal conference. My class in Baghdad became a yoga body prayer hour, so in sixty minutes we repented, we prostrated, and we atoned for peace. After every class, students would look me in the eye and say thank you in their very special way. Lieutenant Colonel Brown, a logistician from up-state New York, always said, in her high-pitched voice, "Thank you . . . I soooo needed this." I would giggle, as she fluffed or patted down her short, fuzzy red hair, which looked the same after as it did before class. Her hair had not changed but energetically she had . . . as I had. Yoga heals.

I had changed a great deal from the moment I stepped on Iraqi soil to my return home in the summer of 2007. I had had many sleepless nights and times of spontane-ous outbursts of frustrating emotions from anger to deep sadness. The first night I visited my parents was about two weeks after returning from Iraq. I had a creepy nightmare and peed in the bed. I was petrified. Under my clever, so cool yogi demeanor I was literally losing it.

During the time I was physically transitioning from war to peace, from Iraq to America, I felt powerless, heartless, and even loveless. I was maintaining my mobilized Army Reserve status by working at the Wounded Soldier and Family Hotline with the Army Human Resources Command in Alexandria, Virginia. I was living one thousand miles away from my sons, who were still attending schools (high school and college) in Gainesville, Florida. At work I was so concerned about the Soldiers and family members who were requesting assistance from the hotline that I forgot my own pain, despair, and need for love from family and friends. Restless in sleep always, my eyes would well up with tears when I least expected it. I was a hot mess. The anxiety attacks threw me under the bus. It took me some time to realize I was not doing a good job of managing and masking my depression. This was my posttraumatic stress growth experience. My yoga practice saved me from drowning in my tears and helped me to survive the haunting residue of war. I decided to teach my brand of B.A.G.H.D.A.D. Yoga at the Human Resources Command building and at my apartment complex. Yoga and the hope for change were ideals that kept me alive and sane. I had the immense love of my family and the calming gift of yoga; with its breath and pause, my tormented Soul was soothed.

According to the Department of Veteran Affairs, an estimated 30 percent of servicemen and -women who return from combat suffer from posttraumatic stress disorder. How a person is affected, as well as how well they cope with the symptoms, will vary. Some symptoms include anger, depression, hypervigilance, flashbacks, nightmares, paralyzing fears, feelings of detachment, irritability, trouble concentrating, and sleeplessness. Though there has always been PTSD, it has only been in the past few years that the military has recognized that it is far better to treat it than to demand that Soldiers "suck it up." Now the military has several assessment programs to recognize the symptoms and changes in behavior that manifest with the disorder in order to take appropriate measures for treatment. The military is also looking for ways to use yoga, acupuncture, virtual reality, and complementary and alternative medicine to treat wounded and ill service members.

Soldiers have returned home in mental disrepair, and though they may look the same on the outside, combat demons are chipping away at their Souls. There have been reports of Soldiers having fits of violent rage, abusing drugs and alcoholic substances, killing their loved ones, or sadly, committing suicide. In 2010, suicides within the military were the highest ever, according to reports from the Department of Defense. Even with the military task forces, 24-hour hotlines and other prevention methods, we have not been able to make the impact needed to change these climbing statistics. Oh, the price of war. We really do need to change.

Getting back to MY new normal after being deployed was a lonely process, although it truly is a journey that one can only take alone. I knew I had changed. I was experiencing St. John of the Cross's "Dark Night of the Soul." I was depressed and dark. This darkness seemed to hover over me, looking for a permanent residence for nearly a year or so. I was wrestling with that son-of-a-bitch big time, I had my boxing gloves on and we duked it out on my yoga mat every day.

Four months after my return home, I went to the Omega Institute in Rhinebeck, New York, for a yoga workshop called "Roots, Rhythm and Soul." It was hosted by legendary Kripalu teacher Maya Breuer and certified yoga teachers Jana Long, Abigail Ifatola Jefferson, Yirser Ra Hotep, and Swami Dinndayal N. Morgan. My then sixty-nine-year-old mother came with me so she could learn that yoga has nothing to do with religion and that it was not going to make her a blasphemous Christian. At times my mother would look at me cock-eyed when I talked in my yoga "ting ting woo-woo" language. Eventually, she understood that yoga's gift was not just in doing some strange movement and bending in places that required the flexibility of Gumby or a contortionist. Neither does yoga require one to chant sounds over and over, denouncing the Bible or religion. I always told her that yoga is life, a union of body, mind, and spirit, and that it can only enliven an already existing relationship with God/Spirit/Universe/Soul/the Formless/Creator/Earth/Pizza/Beer — whatever you wish to call IT. IT is the IT that has power over us perfectly imperfect humans.

During the workshop, I felt the darkness lift, and I figuratively removed my boxing gloves, polished my nails, and lifted my hands and did the spirit-finger wave . . . Jazz hands! I was remembering my roots, my rhythm, and my Soul! We danced to the healing beat of African drums. We laughed, sang chants, and I released the death grip of the shadow. Yoga allowed my body to surrender to the awareness of my spirit and reconnect with others. That was the new normal I wanted, and it was AWESOME!

We met some awesome yogis at the workshop. I had an affinity to Swami Dinndayal, "Master Din." He demonstrated some movement techniques to circulate and harness your individual energies and power based on your personal archetype. He teaches that a person either moves like wind, fire, water, and earth or like animals such as the tiger, cobra, panther, and eagle. Knowing which archetype you represent and its inherent movements, a person can transform stress to empowerment with simple movement techniques.

Master Din told me I moved with the attributes of fire, wind, and the panther, and that I was charismatic, energetic, and agile. I smiled like the Cheshire cat and became instantly intrigued by his teachings. I spoke to him after the workshop about his Yoga Heart Meditative Movement technique and purchased his new book, *Lone Wolf in the Company of Fools and Mystics*. He encouraged me to get a book on numerology as soon as I could and to stay in touch. His manifesto is "you gotta have heart" and I absolutely resonate with that philosophy, since my manifesto is "Live 4 Love" — what else is there anyway, really?

It was my twenty-second year in the military, and in numerology the number 22 is said to be a "master builder" number, which I will explain in detail at the end of this chapter. I love to read and travel. I get my spiritual groove on from reading a myriad of books, attending workshops or conferences and retreats. The annual Whole Life Expo being held in Philadelphia a couple of weeks after the New York Omega workshop would feature two of my most favorite authors and speakers, Marianne Williamson and Deepak Chopra.

I arrived early, so I walked around the large expo-conference area, where there was an inside market place with a variety of vendors selling crystals, organic teas, ten-minute massages for five dollars, astrology readings, and more. I came upon a double-sized booth that was selling books that were neatly displayed across about twelve tables or so. The genres were mixed among the tables, but most of the books were nonfiction titles: *Eco Dog*, *Vegetarian Planet*, *Pilates for the Coreless*, among others. Seeing these titles, I remembered Master Din's advice to find a numerology book. I moseyed along, looking at the stacks of books, musing over the titles as I tried to connect my energy with a title. Finally, I found a book titled *Beginner Numerology*. I excitedly picked it up and headed to the long cashier line that was moving rather slowly. I checked my watch because I had a five-dollar shiatsu massage scheduled and didn't want to miss it. I laid the book back down and made a mental note that there were two of the books that I selected and that one certainly would be there when I returned.

On my way to get my massage, I passed another booth that was selling laminated copies of cheat sheet information cards, like CliffsNotes, on topics such as numerology, chakras, aromatherapy, astrology, and reflexology. I bought the four-by-four-inch plastic numerology card for a mere four dollars, and I bolted to my massage appointment. After my cheap yet effective massage, I sat down to consult my card and to calculate my numerology life path number, which is similar to the idea of astrology but based on the numerical value of your birth date or/and your full birth name.

Using the numerology chart card, I calculated using my birth date of January 2, 1963, and discovered I have a life path of 22, and my full birth name Michele Maudine (ahem — yes, Maudine) Spencer also comes to 22. Ironically, and auspiciously, I have 7 letters in each name: 7,7,7. I recall July 7, 2007, was the biggest wedding date ever. There were so many people including well-known celebrities who had planned to tie the knot on that day in hopes that lucky 7 would wholly protect their matrimony. Some were lucky; some were not!

Here is another interesting mathematical twist on symbolism — well, at least to me — about the numbers 22 and 7: $22 \div 7 = 3.14$ (rounded to two decimal places) or the value of pi (π) when rounded to two decimal places. Since I am not a mathematician, just a voyeur in theories of equations, I referred to the almighty encyclopedia. It defined π as the sixteenth letter in the Greek alphabet, whose value is the ratio of any circle's circumference to its diameter. According to the encyclopedia, it is also an irrational and transcendental number, which means that it cannot be written as the ratio of two integers, and is not constructible. Unlike many physical constants, pi is a dimensionless quantity, meaning that it is simply a number without physical units.

Okay, the truth is, I do not know what all this mathematical mumbo jumbo really means. But I do know that it is important in a number-symbolic kind of a way. Hell, I just think it's cool the way numbers and other signs can teach us more about ourselves, or perhaps confuse us just the same. Either way I know that numbers are awesome portals into our Souls.

Okay, so I read and calculated my life path number from the small laminated numerology card I purchased, and it said that the numbers 11 and 22 are master builder numbers and would not be referred to, only numbers 1 through 9. I became a bit anxious because I calculated that I was a 22. It was suggested that if the reader wanted more in-depth information on numerology to get a specialized book. I immediately returned to the booth of hundreds of books and purchased the *Beginner Numerology* book that I had laid down earlier.

After my purchase, I thumbed to the rear of the book for "Life Path 22" and it was not there. I fingered to the preface and gleaned that this book would not refer the reader to numbers 11 and 22. OK, so now I'm much more eager and agitated. *What in the heck is my vibrational life path number about?* I asked myself. *What is the message here?* I took a deep, deep, calming breath and returned to the book booth and just kind of stood still in front of some random book-covered table. I looked down and saw the heading of a rare book titled *The Key of Destiny*. Another book lay across it like stacked cards, so I couldn't tell what kind of book it was. As if in slow motion, I picked it up and my eyes bugged out of my head

Imagine this, if you can. On the front book cover was a large number 22 and the π symbol above a leafy wreath. A naked woman draped in a lavender shawl that covered her hips and exposed her breasts was standing in the center of the wreath. There were also pictures of an angel, an eagle, a cow and a lion on clouds around the wreath, with two symbols of infinity, one on top and the other below — all of that on the cover of the book. But all I could focus on was the number 22 glaring at me, vibrating.

As I held up the book, I instantly began to sweat and I wanted to wet my pants and scream. I looked around the table at other people scavenging to find their perfect book, to see if I recognized a hidden camera watching me with my mouth gaping, sweat beading on my forehead, and eyes bugging. Nothing. I was in this surreal experience all by myself. I gathered my senses and calmly walked over to the cashier and paid for the book. Its preface was written in 1919. This was dense information on the art and science of numerology. The second page has a symbol that contains the words "Dare Do Keep Silent."

As you can imagine, I was simply awestruck, AWE-mazed, and actually speechless. I do not have the interpretation skills to adequately share or summarize what I learned from *The Key of Destiny*. Besides, it instructed me "do keep silent," so I am mum! However,

I did learn from this about the master builder number 22 from author Hans Decoz in his book *Numerology: Key to Your Inner Self.* He says that "The 22 is the most powerful of all numbers . . . The 22 can turn the most ambitious of dreams into reality. It is potentially the most successful of all numbers . . . It is unlimited, yet disciplined. It sees the archetype, and brings it down to earth in some material form. It has big ideas, great plans, idealism, leadership, and enormous self-confidence . . . It must work toward the realization of goals that are larger than personal ambition. The 22 serves the world in a practical way."

Yep, that last sentence resonates with me. When I read it, I felt greatly honored and motivated. So, I humbly present this book and share my story so that it "may serve the world in a practical way." Lord, I pray that positive change and shifts of energy will continue to inspire our planet. BELIEVE . . . wouldn't that be AWESOME?

During one B.A.G.H.D.A.D. Yoga class, a thoughtful student brought me an ink stamp imprinted with Gandhi's famous quote, "Be the change you want to see in the world," and an inkpad. Inspired, everyone in class received a stamp on the back of their hand, so while in a Forward Fold (*Uttasana*) with nipples "superglued" and pressing on top of your thighs, chillin' with hips just a liftin' and hands touching the floor, those words would become the incentive for digging deeper with their breath, stretching a bit further releasing the backs of the legs, allowing the hamstrings to elongate slowly. In *Uttasana* the head dangles like a bobblehead doll — emptying and changing any negative energy and toxic thoughts. This Forward Fold unfolds the spine; the vertebrae have no choice here but to create space between them. Lengthening, expanding; it's these movements and many more that can manifest the impulse for change within our personal and our collective planetary attitudes . . . oh yes, the AWE-some Audacity of Hope!

W*e're not here to take and we weren't born to indulge. We were born to kneel.*

T. S. Eliot

Kujichagulia (Swahili for "Self-Determination"): *To define ourselves, name ourselves, create for ourselves, and speak for ourselves*

What Is Numerology?

Numerology is based on the idea that everything in the universe has a vibration that correlates to a mathematical number. Like musical notes, we each carry our own unique vibration frequency that resonates at a numerical value. Numerals are everywhere from your cell phone number, address, or license plate, and they affect us subtly — telling us about our current story, our journey, and our history.

A very, very long time ago, great teachers such as Imhotep, Pythagoras, and Plato assigned meanings to certain numbers based on where and how those numbers came up most frequently. Numbers can be used to interpret people's character or divine their future. Using a method analogous to that of the Greek and Hebrew alphabets (in which each letter also represents a number), modern numerology attaches a series of digits to an inquirer's name and uses these, along with the date of birth, to reveal the person's true nature and prospects.

The first consideration of numerology is often the sum of the date of birth. This date, expressed numerically as mm/dd/yyyy, is used to determine what is called the life path number and a variety of other factors in the numerology reading. Reduce the sum of your birth date to a single digit 1 through 9, or to the numerology "master numbers," 11 or 22. These master numbers are not reduced any further. This final number represents who you are at birth and the native traits that you will carry with you through life.

Example: Birthdate of January 2, 1963 (01-02-1963). Add the month (0 + 1) to the day (0 + 2) plus the total of the digits in the year (1 + 9 + 6 + 3). The total sum comes to 22. In my case 22 is a master builder number but can be reduced to 4 (2 + 2); the life path number is 22/4.

Below are some very basic meanings of the life path numbers. If you are as intrigued with this art and science as I am, I encourage reading and researching numerology for there are varying considerations on this subject.

1 Pioneering, independent, creative, original, dominant, leading, impatient

2 Patient, frugal, easy-going, indulgent, intuitive, compromising, patient, cooperative

3 Charming, outgoing, self-expressive, extroverted, energetic, proud

4 Steady, stable, solid, hard-working, dependable

5 Exciting, changeable, seeking new things, visionary

6 Affectionate, conservative, conventional, philanthropic, nurturing

7 Mystical, scholarly, philosophical, reclusive, spiritual, solitary

8 Businesslike, leading, organizing, materialist, status-oriented, power-seeking

9 Humanitarian, intuitive, independent, generous, compassionate, romantic

11 Master builder — A great spiritual person, teacher, and idealist; determined to help others; friendly and genial; may be a perfectionist or a martyr

G

Grow Goodness, Give, Gratitude, Grace . . .
It's ALL God!

Low Push-Up (Chaturanga Dandasana)

Third or Solar Plexus Chakra (Manipura)

Location	Upper abdomen, above the navel, below the chest
Color	Golden yellow
Element	Fire
Sense	Sight
Sound	Me
Functions	Power; digestive processes, metabolism, sympathetic nervous system
Glands or organs	Pancreas, adrenals, stomach, liver, gallbladder
Qualities & lessons	Personal power, ambition, intellect, astral force, desire, will, transformation, self-control, warmth, humor, laughter
Negative qualities	Digestive problems, anger, fear, hate, emphasis on power, frustration, anxiety, perfectionism
Gemstones	Tiger's eye, amber, yellow topaz, peridot

Ashtanga Path
Asana (Physical Discipline)

Army Core Value
Respect

GROW GOODNESS, GIVE, GRATITUDE, GRACE . . . IT'S ALL GOD!

*Look for God. Look for God like a man with his head on
fire looks for water.*

Elizabeth Gilbert

Please take note that it is said that most people live
from only their first three chakras, never ascending to
their fourth, their Heart, and to subsequent chakras.
Some people have glimpses of enlightenment, but for
many, staying low, shallow, small and being rooted in
the material world is their comfort zone. Loftier goals
such as opening the heart, telling the truth, and "being
awake" can be frightening. Imagine living from a place
of compassion, cooperation, integrity, diplomacy, and,
yes, love, as a means to resolving conflicts. Not the ca-
lamitous, back-biting, arrogant, greedy, power-hungry,
and materialist animal nature some people possess.

As in Abraham Maslow's theory of self-actualization, where food and shelter are at the base of the pyramid, to change we all must move from the Soul, our solar plexus, to a place where we can experience more depth. In yoga, we must exhale, release and let go, going lower and hovering, like in *Chaturanga Dandasana*, with strength and power, so we can flow into the next asana, be it Cobra or Upward-Facing Dog, to lift our hearts. The high to low push-up of *Chaturanga* requires not only the strength of your arms to lower the body, but also the potency of the core, so the belly and spine does not collapse on the mat.

You have a choice here. You can go to the knees and then the chest to develop this core strength, ensuring that the elbows are still tucked alongside the body, and lowering the body as a whole. So, when it is time to lift and shift up, the momentum is graceful like a wave. Sometimes, even when you do have the core strength, you might just need to go to your knees, to humble yourself and find strength in prostrating and remembering your dependence on God's grace.

At the end of your practice, place your hands at your heart center with palms together in prayer position, *Anjali Mudra*. (A *mudra* is a hand position.) You do this to honor what comes from your heart and to invoke *namaste* — the Divine in me honors the Divine in you. It is a Sanskrit greeting, words of gratitude, invoking grace.

During my time in Baghdad, I was able to interact with a variety of people. Take, for example, the Nepalese worker who cleaned our offices. He would greet me cheerfully every day with a generous crooked smile of tobacco-stained teeth. I'd look at him, say *"Namaste,"* and wish I could say more, but that was all we needed to understand that we were in this hot mess together. He wore one of those commercial blue jumpsuits that was too large and hid his small frame. He looked like he was in prison working for a chain gang. His dark eyes gleamed when he saw me, and I wondered how long he had been in this foreign country. Would he be able to go back home soon too? Would his tour enable him to make enough money for his family? Was this his seasonal work?

It was rumored that a company hired the Nepalese, Pakistanis, Eastern Indians, and others by telling them they would be working close to their native land, but instead they were sent to Baghdad for an undisclosed amount of time and for questionable wages. So, yes, perhaps this was his prison, since slavery is supposed to be over. I wished he'd find a cruise ship to hustle on; at least he would have a personalized nametag and a uniform that fit properly. This guy had heart, though; he was proud and I understood that. The language of the heart is palpable as it pulsates through tones, whispers, words, silence, and tears.

I know to be grateful every day, for I know how some others live all over this planet; from barrios, ghettos, caves; closets of despair, of hunger, of inhumane filth to magnificent opulence and unfathomable greed . . . I know to say the shortest prayer, "Thank you." Thank you, Lord, for my heart of compassion and what I do have. Being grateful is humbling even when the shit

and the shifting gets funky; many a day in Baghdad I had to force myself to say thank you through my tears. I had to be brave and act in accordance with being a Soldier, a hardened warrior. As a Soul-dier, I shifted my angst to create an awareness and presence of peace while I was Soldiering in the Green Zone, not only through sincerely appreciating the hired help who cleaned our offices and prepared our great meals, but also through my interactions with the Iraqi women who worked at the Iraqi Surgeon General's Office. These women changed my life in more ways I can describe.

How do you Grow Goodness? Give it to the Goddess so she can birth it. The Iraqi women from the Surgeon General's Office and I met for weekly leadership sessions. I began by using my ROTC curriculum notes from when I was teaching at the University of Florida and Georgia Technical Institute. Later, I received some lesson plans from a colleague who was working with the Center of Excellence for Iraqi Leadership for male officers; his leadership course was actually sanctioned by MNSTC-I. My leadership sessions for the Iraqi women, however, were sanctioned by God. I combined what I knew from ROTC with other innovative team-building techniques that I learned over the years to create an empowering, educational, and enlightening format that would inspire our emotional growth.

In one of our first meetings, an Iraqi woman named Wassan, whose nickname was "Violet," asked, "Where is God?" The four women in the room — a dentist, a physical therapist, a secretary, and an Iraqi military policewoman — paused and pondered that BIG tiny question, "Where IS God in all of this mess, this war, anyway?" It is the same question anyone asks when they learn about the atrocities in the world, from the most heinous crimes — parents killing their entire family, a disgruntled employee on a shooting spree, sects of people killing each other because of their heritage: genocide — to catastrophic natural disasters that destroy lives, homes, entire cities, or just the sad pathetic results of poverty, illness, and disease. We ask where God is, I suppose, to separate ourselves from the blame and the inability to correct such complex calamities.

God, the all-powerful and loving one, certainly would NOT let THIS or these things happen. We are in disbelief and want answers to the deranged and the despicable. The fact is, we are interchangeable. We are the Creator — Him/Her — we are made in the Creator's image. We are not separate. Certainly you, the reader, would never do or wish that anything bad would happen to another person. But I believe that our collective fear has produced some God-awful circumstances and consequences. When we sit idly by and while we watch our brother or sister fail and falter although we have the ability to support others, we do not grow our God. When we purposefully insult Mother Earth with toxic waste, or misuse energy and water, what in the ham sandwich are we doing?

We have plundered and ravished too many natural resources. We have kept unethical people in office and corrupt corporations in business far too long. Might I also add again the prevalence and popularity of reality

shows? Are we so simple that we have to watch other people in their lives as a sitcom for entertainment? I do not get that. We must be Present in our own lives. Many people have not led lives in accordance with the Divine, so we need not ask where God is without looking at and asking ourselves what our own personal mission and purpose is while we inhabit this planet, and answering with an action plan to improve it.

After Violet asked "Where is God?" the women from our small group proceeded in a discussion about religion and freedom. Violet was a Christian, which was news to me. I didn't learn in the Army's cultural predeployment briefings on Iraq that in this land of Islam 3 percent of Iraqis were Christian. What we all understood that day was that we are all connected despite religious preference or affiliation. We understood during our conversation that God is everywhere and agreed that all people desire peace, except for those truly sick puppies out there, and that they are the ones who are truly disconnected and feel separate, creating fear and terror.

Our dialogue continued as we discussed the reasons for the war, the want for miracles and for amnesty. Some of the women asked practical questions like "How can I get a visa?" and impractical ones such as "Will you help me get out of the country?" We segued to less serious topics and debated about the best kohl eyeliner, raising our children, men, love, romance, sex, jeans from The Gap, and Victoria's Secret lingerie. I learned that my new Iraqi friends, my Sistagurls, had easy access to the Internet and were quite adept in using it. I saw how they "instant messaged" each other as they worked. Of course, I wondered what would they IM to each other in this war-toiled land. Here's an imagined IM session:

Me: Did you hear THAT one last night?

Sistagurl: No, I slept through it . . .

Me: You know the other day, when I was making my chai tea, a bullet landed in my hummus.

Sistagurl: Nooooooo, really? Oh, that's nothing. This morning, shrapnel flew into my window while I was combing my baby's hair and just missed us by INCHES.

Me: Wow. Guess,what? I had an hour's use from my generator today. My husband stood in line for eight hours to get two gallons of gas.

Sistagurl: You are soooo lucky!

Me: No, we are both lucky. We are still alive.

Terrorism, for instance, is not our deepest problem, but rather the effect of a deeper one. Hatred itself is our deepest problem. While military power might contain the terrorists, only love has the power to dismantle the hate from which terrorism emerges. There is no problem to which the love of God — manifest in our love for each other — is not the ultimate solution. Yet we must look for that love within ourselves. A nation that puts money before love must address that problem first if we wish miracles to bless and protect us. It's not the word God, but the work of God, that is necessary in order to call forth miracles.

Marianne Williamson

My Iraqi Sistagurls showed me several Arabic websites. I was so impressed because, with my American arrogance and ignorance, I thought the majority of Islamic women were oppressed and that they accepted their plight, but oppression is not synonymous with ignorance. I knew that together, in these weekly meetings, we would be able to learn a lot from each other and share our similar yet different cultures.

I taught the women about leadership from a military perspective, and also from the perspective of a creative community art-ivist. We decided we needed to have an action plan, a platform to validate our sublime power and purpose of working together. With the support of my superior officer, I spearheaded the first International Women's Day Celebration on Phoenix Base at the DFAC. International Women's Day is always held on March 8. Since 1911, this global day celebrates the economic, political, and social achievements of women past, present, and future.

The theme of our celebration was "Women with Voices," giving a voice to the words that expressed power over the fear, pain, and the lost hopes and dreams that were buried under the rumble and ash of war. I felt our collective voices could shepherd in love, peace, and empowerment over the oppression. The strength of our compassion created a venue for all of the women to discover themselves through an innovative creative use of none other than Mrs. Potato Head.

Yes, it was Mrs. Potato Head that came to me in a vision after a nightly mortar attack. You see, Mrs.

or Mr. Potato Head metaphorically and symbolically can be ANY one of us. This favorite childhood toy has many parts; these parts can be put in any hole of its body. For example, an arm for a nose, eyes for a mouth — no judgment, just saying. As dysfunctional as it is, an arm can stay in an eyehole forever. The deal here is, we too can choose how we live and put our parts and pieces together. Using Mrs. Potato Head at International Women's Day was going to be an interactive creative experience to show how to find God and grow Goodness.

"Women with Voices" would not only celebrate our American-Iraqi collaboration but also showcase that even in the heat of battle, in the center of fire, there is gold. As women, we are rich, vulnerable, and worthy. We can glow through the darkness together, as women before us did in their bouffants and miniskirts, wearing afros and burning their bras. Women through "herstory" have clawed their way out of the kitchen to the boardroom as a CEO or to the cockpit of a fighter jet. The suffrage movement and the Civil Rights movement made the way for women of all ethnic and racial groups to seek equality and justice for all.

The Soul of the Solar Plexus, the third chakra, has the heat and power within it for MOVEMENT — ascension and acceptance to the Heart, the fourth chakra. For our International Women's Day celebration, our movement, I enlisted the help of a few female colleagues, both officer and enlisted from the Air Force, the Army, and the Marines. They helped decorate, moderate, and dance. One female Fijian guard sang a native song from her country; she was accompanied by another guard who strummed a ukulele. A Polynesian Air Force major danced a perfect hula. The tables were adorned with centerpiece photographs of great "wild" women who changed the world, such as Susan B. Anthony, who fought for women's right to vote; Benazir Bhutto, the first female prime minster of Pakistan; Corazon Aquino, the first female Philippine president; and the big "O" — Oprah.

We began the event by singing the American and Iraqi national anthems. A PowerPoint picture slide show of women from around the world played on the DFAC wall from a computer and projector. Several pictures for the slides were taken from the enlightening book *The Other Side of War*, authored by Zainab Salbi. After the anthems, Major Anderson read the beautiful and poignant poem featured in the book, which was eloquently written by Alice Walker:

> What is happening
> in Africa
> (& elsewhere)
> is because
> the men
> did not listen
> to the women
> & the women
> did not listen
> to the women

either
& because
the people did not listen
to each other
& themselves
& because
nobody listened
to the children
&
the poets.
                    Alice Walker

"Women with Voices" enabled us to *listen* to our Soul . . . it was truly a powerful event. We had more than eighty participants, about half were Iraqi and the others were proud military women serving in the Green Zone.

Now, what about my vision of using Mrs. Potato Head?

In the middle of the program, an announcement was made in the style of CNN's Cooper Anderson: "Late breaking news. Mr. Potato Head had been captured by extremist terrorists, a gang of fries called the Oil Canola!" (Please use your imagination for this reenactment.) The program moderator stopped as a news flash came abruptly on the PowerPoint screen, with a male anchor stating that Mr. Potato Head was being held hostage and could only be saved if Mrs. Potato Head rescued him. Yes, women save men, stand behind them, and make them "good."

As the program's hostess-with-the-mostest, I

explained to the confused women that Mrs. Potato Head was distraught and just in pieces (literally) over the news of her husband's capture, but she must get herself "together" to save her man. On cue, my assistants placed one toy box of Mrs. Potato Head on each table. I gave the rules of engagement for the game, which were that the women MUST work collectively together to put Mrs. Potato Head together, there would be absolutely no talking, and that every table MUST finish together. I said, "Time is of the essence before Mr. Potato is peeled and fried! Ready, set, GO!"

Of course, the Americans knew this toy, so the familiar parts went into the right holes very easily. But then, the women realized that there were duplicate and missing parts from the box, so lo and behold an arm finally went in an eyehole, wrong answer. So where were the right pieces — the arms, feet, hats, noses, purses? I had a picture of the perfect, "whole," Mrs. Potato Head on the PowerPoint screen so the women could match the proper look for accuracy. Every completed Mrs. Potato Head fashionista had to have the matching handbag and shoes.

The "no talking" rule was enforced, laughing and giggles aside. The women worked feverishly, and they waved arms and pointed to extra spare parts and empty holes at other group tables. One table of women confidently negotiated the correct parts and raised their WHOLE Mrs. Potato Head in the air, claiming to be the winner. But I reminded the enthusiastic women that, according to the rules of engagement, EVERYONE must finish together to win. Soon after, the women at each of the tables all matched pieces and parts to the correct holes and completed their perfect Mrs. Potato Head. Yes, the spirit of collaboration and cooperation — GRACE!

The lesson learned was that although we were only tables apart, or countries apart, it is in our best interest to cross the aisle, the seemingly great divide, to share our extra arm or hat so we can all have feet. Until we are ALL put together, we will not be whole. Divided, we can't save our men, our children, or our planet. We must move from powerlessness to be women of strength who can shift to love and grow with God.

CNN's Heidi Collins interviewed me that evening about the celebration. It aired in the U.S. the following morning, since Baghdad is seven hours ahead of the U.S. East Coast and eleven hours ahead of West Coast time. I was so excited and nervous to speak LIVE on CNN! No one prepped me on possible questions or how to direct and control my message. Surely the message and significance of "Women with Voices" was recogniz-ing the gifts of women and their power to transform the landscape of war. But when Heidi asked the question about working with Iraqi women, "What areas do they need help with the most? What are they really reaching out for?" I drew a blank.

I thought to myself, *Shucks, they want what ALL women want: health, clean parks for their kids, new*

panties, fresh water, thinner thighs, and men who can actively listen and pick up their own dirty clothes. And since you're asking, can ya please hold off on the bombs for a while, why don't cha?! I paused for what seemed to be an hour and fiddled with the sound earpiece thingie that was giving me delayed feedback. I finally asked her to repeat the question, and answered, "I believe just more belief in themselves. I mean, they definitely have a lot of hope for their country, but they want to have their voices heard!" Now wasn't that a novel idea? Brilliant, actually . . . "Voices heard." Patronizing, I know. I hoped I didn't sound like a goof, but I wanted us to be rescued from this war.

Heidi asked a few more questions before she asked me the true zinger and highlight of my five-minutes-of-fame CNN interview. "You're involved in a different kind of work that does help U.S. troops . . . and that's yoga . . ." she said. And I lit up like a Christmas tree on steroids when she made that statement. I already had a 1,000-watt smile so my grin and grill probably could have shined a hole through the studio ceiling, it was so bright and cheesy. I was crystal clear on that answer and why I was teaching yoga. I said, "Yeah! BaghdadYoga.com — You know, if you're not reflective about what you can do here, wherever that you are, and help out, you know, you're missing a great opportunity . . . we breathe together, so that the energy can definitely change. And collectively there's so much power that we can do energetically." My heart was pounding out of my chest, I knew I had stuttered, cheesed all over the camera — melting it, but most of all, I was able to share OUR story. Yessss, can you hear me?!

Wouldn't you know it, The Beast reared its ugly head the next day and I was reprimanded for saying "BaghdadYoga.com," reprimanded as though I were selling some limited-time-only Baghdad vacation timeshare with a guaranteed "fun or your money back" clause. "Call today or just go to baghdadyoga.com to reserve your hooch and get your WTF AUM on! Hurry . . . free Warrior poses while they last!" Nothing in my live CNN interview came close to advertising a year's stay in bombed-out Baghdad. The Beast didn't HEAR that I was sharing the powerful rich history of women that crossed cultures and nations, all it heard was "Blah, blah, blah BAGHDADYOGA.COM, blah, blah, blah women."

Certainly after that day, I stayed low-key. I would be returning home within two months, and I needed to stay drama-free. Even after the success of the woman's program and a month later being recognized on Paul Zahn's weekly show "People You Should Know" on CNN for reaching out to Iraqi women, The Beast downgraded my coveted Bronze Star Medal to a Joint Service Commendation Medal, and I was not allowed at the formal farewell that the MNSTC-I commander hosted. I was emotionally distraught and confused over being penalized for sharing my sincere, beautiful global work. Absolutely no senior officer pushed The Beast off me; they acquiesced. I was basically told, "Suck it up, get over it, and drive on, Soldier." I was crushed, not because I didn't receive the Bronze Star but because I felt our Army values were not adhered to. I am grateful for my service, believe you me. It just felt like a slap in the face to my commitment and service while I witnessed others receive the Bronze Star for only being in country for six months, making coffee, hating the Iraqis, and never leaving the FOB. Ludicrous how the award system worked and what the leadership permitted.

I was forced to shift my angst. I came to appreciate my Joint Service Commendation Medal because the words can stand alone on their own merit: JOINT (Unity, Together) SERVICE (*Seva*, Purpose) COMMENDATION (Praise, Honor). Yeah, the Bronze Star has more perceived weight and sits higher on the military uniform but MY award decorates ME from the inside out . . . and It's name is GOD . . . nanny, nanny, boo, boo, take THAT, Beast!

Now let's lift and shift to our hearts, roll your shoulders back . . . remembering that the movement from *Chaturanga Dandasana* is that high to low push-up with core strong and firm, elbows tucked into the sides, and propelling you to your next asana of choice, Cobra or Upward-Facing Dog. Depending on your upper strength, suppleness of the spine, or even just what you may be feeling or needing, move with grace and certainty that your signature flow is how you grow to God. Ready? Set? Go . . . Inhale, lift, and shine your Heart!

The Attitude of Gratitude is the highest yoga.

Yogi Bhajan

Ujima (Swahili for "Collective Work and Responsibility"): *To build and maintain our community together and make our brothers' and sisters' problems our problems and to solve them together*

H

HEAL Your Heart, Our Planet . . .
Harmony: Happy!

Cobra (Bhujangasana) or
Upward-Facing Dog (Urdhva Mukha Svanasana)

Fourth or Heart Chakra (Anahata)

Location	Center of the chest, at level of the heart
Color	Green or pink
Element	Air
Sense	Feeling, touch
Sound	Fa
Functions	Compassion; anchors the life force from the Higher Self, energizes the body with the life force, blood circulation
Glands or organs	Heart, thymus gland, circulatory system, arms, hands, lungs
Qualities & lessons	Divine or unconditional love, forgiveness, compassion, understanding, oneness with life, harmony, contentment, acceptance, peace, openness, harmony, contentment, balance
Negative qualities	Repression of love, emotional instability, heart problems, circulation problems, abandonment, fear, sadness, anger, resentment, jealousy, hostility
Gemstones	Emerald, tourmaline, malachite, green aventurine, jade, rose quartz, rhodonite

Ashtanga Path
Pranayama (Life Energy-Breathing)

Army Core Value
Selfless Service

Four

HEAL YOUR HEART, OUR PLANET . . . HARMONY: HAPPY!

I am the Self existent in the heart of all beings.
Bhagavad Gita

Opening your heart and living from a place of compassion is as rewarding as it can be dangerous. At the heart of ANYTHING is the life force and its essence. In our very bodies, our heart skillfully pumps blood and oxygen throughout our organs and tissues, our flesh and bones, so we may live. It is said that the longest distance on earth remains the twelve inches from the human brain to the human heart. Thinking so much with our head, analyzing and rationalizing or even irrationalizing everything to the nth degree sometimes doesn't allow our hearts to open and surrender for serendipity to take place in our lives.

The fun and adventure of this human form is to play and risk. When it comes to matters of the heart, you never really lose nor can it ever be lost . . . because

Love just is. We are here to LOVE and that is the truth of the matter. The matter of the heart is what we are here to do on this planet, to love unconditionally and to live harmoniously and to live for love. It is the greatest gift you can share. There is no monetary value for love . . . it is spiritually priceless.

Dan Millman, author of *Way of the Peaceful Warrior,* says he calls himself a peaceful warrior "because the battles we fight are on the inside." When a person lives from their heart, they are not only peaceful warriors but also spiritual gangsters. Such people are fueled by the ethereal essence that gangs up on their dark nights and make them light. The light illumines the space in which God, the Divine, dwells. Jesus was that essence; he was a lamp to light the way. My very own mother, Geri, has always been my guiding light.

My mother is a visionary and trendsetter in the Bakersfield community. Her hair and beauty salon was appropriately named The Pacesetter, which speaks volumes about my favorite matriarch. Her example groomed me for a successful military career as Warrior. My mother constantly set the pace for creativity and community service for me. As a child, she served as my troop leader for my first uniformed service in Bluebirds, the Camp Fire program for younger girls. She served as the PTA president at McKinley Elementary School for several years and participated as a board member in so many councils, committees, and community organizations that I doubt she remembers them all. My mother has always been the wind beneath my wings so I could soar to greater heights.

After raising my brothers Michael and John and being married for more than fifty years to my father John, my mother, now seventy-four years old, claims she is in her sexy seventies! My mom shares her heart freely and champions senior citizens in her community by educating them about heart disease, breast cancer, and smoking cessation. She established a nonprofit organization called Sisters Getting Fit to encourage women, especially seniors, to embrace a healthier lifestyle.

My mother, like many other people who do extraordinary things, is making a positive difference to heal our planet. All spiritual warriors carve a path for others to follow. The warrior inspires and teaches us how to create our own legacy. Our living legacy is our "dash." Your dash is the mark etched on your tombstone; it is that itsy-bitsy line between the day you were born and the day your spirit leaves this earth. Your dash represents everything that you are, were, wanted to be, and could have been. Our legacy is completely ours, uniquely crafted entirely by us. May we be mindful of our dash always; may that minuscule line on our tombstone be the depiction of the ginormous contribution from how we led our lives, not the retraction of what we withheld.

Let my Soul smile through my heart and my heart smile through my eyes, that I may scatter rich smiles in sad hearts.

Paramahansa Yogananda

I cannot emphasize enough that the goal of the spiritual journey is not to walk on water or attempt to turn water into wine as Jesus did. One mustn't even sit in the lotus posture under the bodhi tree like the young prince Siddhartha, the Buddha, and vow not to rise from meditation until attaining perfect enlightenment. It is our everyday intentions and actions that matter. For instance, when you drive your vehicle, how about letting the car blinking its turning signals at your side get in front of you without huffing and puffing in road rage? This open-heart procedure is NOT surgery; it is showing respect, doing good, and being a steward of peace.

Opening your heart as a peaceful warrior is as simple as reading to a child, mentoring a co-worker, or being a nonjudgmental listening ear to a friend. It is bringing your own grocery bags to the store for your weekly routine of shopping, changing to eco-friendly lightbulbs, and stopping smoking. It is turning off the television and tuning into a great book that speaks to your heart and Soul. Opening your heart is writing a thank-you note to a person you've been meaning to contact for more than a month or two or three — years! It is turning the corners of your mouth up when the monkeys start climbing on your back and your breath stutters in shallow spurts. Stop, breathe deep, let peace in, forgive and allow your heart to open. Be grateful for your gifts, whatever they are, and share them for FREE.

My dear first cousin Toni has coached girls' basketball for years. Now with her nonprofit, Givin' Back 2

Da Game, her legacy and love for coaching girls' basketball parlays into mentoring and building teamwork. The organization helps girls develop a work ethic and leadership traits. It instills self-esteem and provides opportunities for these young athletic girls to be inspired and motivated to attend college by earning scholarships to further their education and their athletic prowess.

Your time as a peaceful spiritual warrior can be one solitary conscious breath a day, or multiple actions that culminate into a symphony of healing awareness and harmony. What matters is that you are present and are being the change, holding the space for others to recognize and honor your legacy while you are alive on this planet.

The journey of courage is what we are all traveling. My "bestest" prayer is the Serenity Prayer.

> God grant me the Serenity to accept the things
> I cannot change,
> The Courage to change the things I can,
> AND the WISDOM to know the difference.

When I have worked myself into some tizzy, spinning out of control, fighting the committee in my head, not listening to my heart, it is then that I don't breathe. I need to be with my emotions and say that sweet short prayer to move out the paralyzing "freak out" session with myself. For me, prayer helps me mid-spin to balance and cease the monkey-mind madness so I can collect myself and Be Still and Know God.

There were few women left in the Iraqi military when I arrived in Baghdad, so I was fortunate enough to have worked, played, listened, laughed, cried, and journeyed with them. To my knowledge, they only worked within the Iraqi Surgeon General's Office. Major Angham, one of the keynote speakers at the International Women's Day program that I spoke of earlier, lived within the Green Zone perimeter with her only son, who went to a private school "outside" in the Red Zone.

(Let me digress a bit, but isn't it ironic? The color green is the chakra for the heart, full of compassion, and the color red, the root chakra, is the base for safety and security. Can we ever reach to open our hearts in a real way without having a strong safe stabilizing foundation? So was the Green Zone really *green* or was it *red*? Just musing!)

Major Angham was the highest-ranking female in the Iraqi military. In 2003, the first class of military women went to basic training in Jordan. A video documentary, *Journey of Courage*, was created about their experience. I have pictures of the graduating class and a woman all decked out in her Islamic dress navigating an obstacle course — very impressive! Their military training was eight weeks long and very similar to American basic training. The class produced eighty-eight graduates. There has not been another class since then because several women have been assassinated, exiled, or mutilated.

Major Angham retold accounts of the assassinations and of arms being chopped off rather matter-of-factly. I thought of the pain she probably held in her heart to continue to lead from such an isolating place. The Iraqi political climate had changed and the absence of women in the process weakened the country. Even during Saddam's reign, women were not as marginalized as they were when I served in Baghdad. They held positions in the various ministries (political departments), which gave them visibility within the government. The sad state of affairs at the time then was that women's fear and the oppression got the best of them.

In dire straits, they needed a militia of their own to assist in returning them to a place of respect, honor, and power for the healing of their country and our planet. Oppression is not synonymous with ignorance; my Iraqi women friends were incredibly talented and intelligent — courageous and peaceful.

Major Angham, because she lived in the Green Zone, wore her military uniform every day. Others, like Lieutenant Reem, rarely, if ever, wore theirs. Lieutenant Reem wore her regular Islamic dress, covered arms with long sleeves and hijab headdress. But she lived in the Red Zone, as did Violet, who wore typical traditional American-style outfits. The women shared with me that living in the Red Zone and working in the Green Zone required an arduous daily journey. There were early-morning struggles to get a taxi or secure an inconspicuous ride, which were both very hazardous.

The women's routes had to change often so the anti-American Iraqis could not follow them and identify them as conspirators with their American guests. To be identified as a conspirator was dangerous. Working in the Surgeon General's Office was a relatively safe haven and provided a decent salary for these educated women.

The lesson from Women with Voices, the International Women's Day program that we held in celebration of Women's History Month, was that our her-story has been one of mistaken identity. The goddess, the witch, and other forms of the divine feminine have been vilified for centuries, and today atrocities continue against women. Though women are no longer burnt at the stake, as Joan of Arc and other women who were deemed to be in possession of earthly powers such as keen intuition were, there are modern-day assaults, such as genital mutilation, sexual slavery, abuse, rape, and forced prostitution. When we live from our heart center we can recognize what needs to be addressed so women no longer suffer and our divine Mother Earth will not retaliate with her wrath. Atonement is the remedy, an elixir for peace.

What we don't engage we cannot transform.

Marianne Williamson

Zainab Salbi, a yogini and founder of Women for Women International, an American nonprofit organization, knows all too well about hope and heart. She is an author of several books. Her book *The Other Side of War* speaks about women and their oppression in war and what will become of all of us if women's voices are not heard. Interestingly enough, Salbi was born and raised in Baghdad, and her father was Saddam Hussein's private pilot. She escaped to the United States, went on to further her higher education goals, and made it her life mission to speak for women who otherwise would not be heard. Her organization has helped women in nine countries with microlending, education, and more. Since its inception in 1993, Women for Women International has been serving socially excluded women in conflict and post-conflict countries by advocating that engaging women is the most effective avenue toward creating lasting change and stability within a society. "Stronger Women Build Stronger Nations" is one of its slogans.

Across the globe, undeclared wars and internal armed conflicts have reached an unprecedented number. There have been more than 250 major wars since the end of World War II, resulting in over 23 million casualties. Modern warfare is no longer confined to battlefields. Around the world, non-combatants are finding themselves in the direct line of fire, suffering greatly and becoming the anonymous and undercounted casualties of violent conflicts. In today's wars, 90 percent of casualties are civilians, 75 percent of whom are women and children; a century ago, 90 percent of war casualties were male Soldiers. As never before, women are disproportionately affected by war and civil strife. Women are targeted for ethnic cleansing and subjected to rape as a tool of war. They lose male family members who leave to fight and are killed. Many are displaced from their own homes. When widowed by war, they are thrust into the role of sole provider, often without marketable skills or a viable means to earn an income and often in communities that do not value their place in society.

From *The Other Side of War* by Zainab Salbi

As the first viable woman candidate of the United States to make her bid for the presidency, in 2008 former first lady Hillary Clinton proved proudly and confidently through her campaign that she was fiercely competitive. I respected her tenacity as a wife, mother, and daughter. Her journey is also a demonstration of what is possible. In one of her last campaign speeches, she passionately stated, "Although we weren't able to shatter that highest, hardest glass ceiling this time, thanks to you, it's got about 18 million cracks in it . . . And the light is shining through like never before, filling us all with the hope and the sure knowledge that the path will be a little easier next time."

It may not be easier, Hillary, now our honorable Secretary of State, but certainly the path may be a bit wider with fewer potholes. I'm willing to predict that within the next two elections, a woman will earn the position of president of our nation. May she represent this great land with her heart and speak and live the truth, for nothing less will be tolerated.

We will not go from President Obama's motto of "hope and change" to a hipless skirt. Our first female president must be well-rounded and curved with culture, otherwise what we have will be some boring suit and a waste of fabric. She needs to be *fierce*! Prepared. Her matching handbag to save Mother Earth has to be filled to the rim with accessories: a notched belt with a buckle that has a Super-Mutha button on it, tweezers that can pluck BS from some terrorist stronghold, and heels high enough that when you throw them they boomerang and return to her oversized designer handbag. Of course, she will need plenty of Band-Aids from all the paper cuts she will get from changing ancient policies that kept Obama's "hope and change" from fully manifesting. And finally, she will need a good stapler to assault the naysayers by stapling their forehead to their heart!

Without connecting to our heart and fully inculcating the essence of compassion for our planet to heal, it will not spin on its own axis harmoniously. It will continue to spin out of control unconsciously into oblivion, degreening everything, living in the red, in fear and exiled from love. Hell. Being eco-friendly and eco-wise, we keep our heart warm and open to shift the trend of global warming to healing.

When we lift our chest, our heart center in Cobra or in Upward-Facing Dog by using the strength of our arms and the flexibility in our back, lengthening and creating space in our spine, we open to the potentiality and possibilities for all types of healing. This slight back-bending move generates that Egyptian sphinx appearance, readying for the powerful and dynamic move of the Dawg — Downward-Facing Dog — while our *dristi*, which is our gaze, looks up and out. Truth focused. Shoulder blades slide back and down, forcing the chest to lift and open all four chambers of the heart: healing.

Imagine making that giant twelve-inch leap of faith from our head to our hearts, to what ails our planet and us. Imagine allowing compassion to fill the spaces that may be empty and dark. Imagine further charging our "light" muscles; shining, strengthening our wisdom bones, and powering up our activism forces within our communities. May our hearts beat to the healing rhythm of the Soul force as a peaceful warrior: a spiritual gangster, in unison and in harmony. Being Happy!

The willingness with which our young people are likely to serve in any war, no matter how justified, shall be directly proportional to how they perceive how the veterans of earlier wars were treated and appreciated by their nation.

George Washington

Ujamaa (Swahili for "Cooperative Economics"): *To build and maintain our own stores, shops, and other businesses, and to profit from them together*

"Hurry up and wait" at Fort McCoy, Wisconsin, June 2006

In full battle rattle, Kuwait, June 2006

Showing Gator Pride, Phoenix Forward Operating Base, 2006

At the Liberty Pool with Andrea Parhamovich (killed in action January 17, 2007), December 2006

International Women's Day with Major Gina Anderson (right), March 8, 2007

L-R: Lieutenant Reem, unnamed, Wassan (Violet), February 2007

At the dining facility with Lieutenant Reem

With M. J. Abbit after the last yoga class, May 2007

With Major Angham, the highest-ranking female Iraqi officer, May 2007

D

DIGNITY, Discipline, DEEPEN Your Faith, Your Love, Your LIFE!

Downward-Facing Dog: (Adho Muka Svanasana)

Fifth or Throat Chakra (Vishuddha)

Location	Throat area
Color	Blue
Element	Ether or atmosphere; the higher expression of all signs
Sense	Hearing
Sound	Sol
Functions	Communication; understanding of both verbal and mental communications, speech, sounds, vibration
Glands or organs	Thyroid gland, throat and jaw areas, alimentary canal, lungs, vocal cords, the breath
Qualities & lessons	Speaking up, releasing, healing, power of the spoken word, any creative expression, peace, truth, loyalty, honesty, integrity
Negative qualities	Uptightness, low self-esteem, low self-confidence, hostility, anger, resentment, ignorance, lack of discernment, depression, thyroid problems
Gemstones	Blue lace agate, lapis lazuli, sodalite, turquoise

Ashtanga Path
Pratyahara (Withdrawal of senses) — managing body chemistry, compulsiveness, perception vs. instinctual action

Army Core Value
Honor

Five

DREAM, DISCIPLINE, DEEPEN YOUR FAITH, YOUR LOVE, YOUR LIFE, DIGNITY

The goal of life is to make your heartbeat match the beat of the universe, to match your nature with Nature.
Joseph Campbell

We all love heroes. Heroes like Captain America, Captain Crunch, Superman, Wonder Woman, Rudolph the Red-Nosed Reindeer, Lassie, and Luke in *Star Wars*. We are heroes too; whether we know it or not, we all are embarking on a journey with a fantastic voyage.

In the book *The Hero with a Thousand Faces*, Joseph Campbell, the late prolific mythology and spiritual teacher and author, who, by the way, coined the phrase "follow your bliss," eloquently shares the story about the "hero's journey." Campbell said that the journey comprises a series of stages. Among these stages are hearing the call to adventure, crossing the threshold, facing tests and ordeals, gaining the reward, being transformed, and returning home with a gift.

I first discovered Dr. Campbell's work in 1999, twelve years after his death and after a long Army Reserve battle assembly (drill) weekend. An Army Reserve Soldier, or weekend warrior, can select a Reserve center that has a unit that uses their particular skill in their immediate local area or choose to travel further to meet the needs of their position and rank. As a medical service officer, my specialties at the time were patient administration and preventive medicine. My unit was the 345th Combat Support Hospital (CSH) in Jacksonville, Florida. As a first lieutenant I was the company commander at the hospital's subordinate unit in Gainesville.

After seven years as a Reserve officer, I was promoted to captain, and I felt the seven-year itch to change and embark on other opportunities to serve more fully and to follow my bliss . . . wherever that would be. I just knew I needed a new unit, a new Army family.

My first overseas deployment with the CSH was just two weeks in Guatemala in the Mayan jungle of the Petén. This humanitarian Medical Readiness Training Exercise (MEDRETE) mission opened my eyes to how nearly half of the world lives in abject poverty. A medical team of about twenty CSH personnel with a range of specialties set up an ad hoc medical clinic in an elementary school in Flores. We were escorted to the small colorful town by armed men from the Guatemalan army; we had to pass the beautiful shores of Lake Petén Itzá that seemed to serve as a laundry, bathing area, and playground for the locals. I don't remember any fishermen; was that a sign?

The majority of the townsfolk that we saw had parasitic worms. My job was to teach families preventive medicine or personal hygiene basics, such as hand washing before eating and after using the bathroom. It was a creative task since there was limited running water. One bucket of water might be used for their dirty dishes and clothes, and then for the body. As for soap, it was a luxury, as were shoes for many of the indigenous people. Many parasites entered through the soles of the people's feet, not to mention the households are accustomed to sharing the dirt floor of their tin and cardboard shanty homes with the family chickens and pigs.

Our medical team was not prepared to treat such a large population for parasites. We eventually ran out of the proper medication and resorted to handing out prenatal vitamins. I never saw such gratitude for a large pink pill that would do little to nothing, acting as a placebo. We saw almost a thousand people over a five-day period. For some it was their first time seeing a real physician, dentist, or veterinarian. They came from miles away, dressed up as if they were going to an award ceremony, a christening, a wedding, or their first prom — somewhere other than a makeshift Army clinic in the jungle.

However they came and however they appeared, we greeted the weary travelers and locals enthusiastically and provided the best medical care we could. I felt so proud to be of service; we were their heroes, even for that brief time. The fact is that the Army conducts humanitarian missions all over the world to help impoverished townships. I just wish we did more human building than power bombing.

While in Guatemala I had the supreme pleasure of visiting the splendid Mayan ruins of Tikal. I had a very mystical spiritual experience as I hiked among these massive ancient structures dating back to around 600 B.C. I felt a shift, an opening — perhaps an awakening to our Mother Earth like never before. I truly felt like I was beginning to embark on a journey of no return. I was hearing the hero's call to an adventure. I had to be courageous, be a hero in my life and save it.

My senses and emotions filled my eyes with tears of awe and gratitude during my Mayan ruin hike. At that time I was reading the book *Women Who Run with the Wolves* by Dr. Clarissa Pinkola Estés. The book was changing my life with every story she told; "The craft of questions, the craft of stories, the craft of the hands — all these are the making of something, and that something is soul. Anytime we feed soul, it guarantees increase," she wrote.

Was that what I was experiencing, an *increase* in my Soul on top of those monolithic structures? This increase was not some scary, hairy, gnawing, four-eyed worm working its way from my brain to my belly to hatch a million baby parasites, this increase was my hero's journey having my Soul bliss out!

My core expanded and my heart grew strength after the MEDRETE. And when I returned home to my family — a husband, two growing boys, and a mixed-breed dog named Taz — my life as a wife as I knew it would change. I had released the wolf, ate the worm — no tequila necessary — and my increased spirit broke free. My heartbeat matched the beat of the Universe.

When women reassert their relationship with the wildish nature, they are gifted with a permanent and internal watcher, a knower, a visionary, an oracle, an inspiratrice, an intuitive, a maker, a creator, an inventor, and a listener who guide, suggest, and urge vibrant life in the inner and outer worlds. When women are close to this nature, the fact of that relationship glows through them. The wild teacher, wild mother, wild mentor supports their inner and outer lives, no matter what.

Dr. Clarissa Pinkola Estés

Now, it wasn't a matter of choice anymore to not follow my bliss. I had to speak my truth about what was going on inside me. I had no name for it then, but later learned it was an "awakening" and it was a "deepening" of my faith. I had what many would assert was "a good husband." He had a Ph.D., for Pete's sake! He had a good job with benefits, and was a conscientious father who loved his family and his in-laws. My husband helped with the laundry, cooked sometimes, and was an excellent lover. He hardly ever hung out at night with his homeboys. He played golf on Sundays, he always kissed me when he came home from work, and he loved me. But I wanted a divorce with a quickening. I didn't know why I was with him anymore. Where did the love go? The connection? What in the hell was happening to me? I had the golden handcuffs of marriage on and I wanted them off. Now. I wanted out even if I had to chew my arm off. I knew I was in my shadow, and I was certain that I had to leave my marriage. My journey within and without was waiting. I was being peeled alive, and

I didn't know how to stop it. Actually, I didn't want it to stop. The breakdown would lead me to a breakthrough. I was eager and afraid, but I had to peel every layer as if my life depended on my being raw and weepy.

As for my Reserve duty assignment with the Combat Support Hospital, that too had to be exorcised after the MEDRETE. Now as a true *wild woman* following my bliss, I became disgruntled about the training support I was receiving from the commander, and I scheduled an interview with the 478th Civil Affairs Battalion, located six hours away in South Miami. The civil affairs mission was the olive branch — it is that part of the Army that does civil military and humanitarian work to use more diplomacy to win the hearts and minds of our victims, our prey, our allies, and our friends. The 478th CAB invited me into their world and I transferred lickety-split. I howled loudly, as a wolf might do when set free.

It should be noted here that an Army Reserve and National Guard Soldier is no longer just a weekend warrior, since their duties extend far beyond and throughout the month. Their efforts and commitment as "twice the citizen" are commendable. Reserve Soldiers work part- or full-time jobs, or perhaps go to school in addition to serving their country when she calls. It is virtually impossible to complete all the tasks that are required of Soldiers in just one weekend and two weeks out of the year. Since 9/11, our operational tempo has increased tenfold. So much is required, and yearlong deployments have stressed our Soldiers to the max, affecting both their families and their professional civilian careers.

Reserve Soldiers have the challenging responsibility to balance these priorities. Their call to service may be passé to some, and we sometimes may not get the respect we deserve from our big brother, the active-duty Soldier, but any call to service deserves respect, from our public school teachers, police officers, fire fighters, council members, and community board members to plain little ole YOU. I deeply respect YOU, my hero. Thank YOU for YOUR Service!

*T**he only real voyage of discovery consists not in seeking new landscapes but in having new eyes.*

Marcel Proust

The deepening of my faith, my life, and my love resulted in a monthly six-hour one-way commute to South Florida for my Reserve drill when I transferred to the civil affairs unit. I normally stayed on Homestead Airbase in Perrine, Florida. Sometimes the rooms were hard to reserve because the rate was only $21 a night. Many weekends I wasn't so fortunate and the standard $75-plus per night at a local hotel would apply. My pay at that time was only about $250 per weekend, so I was spending more than half on gas, hotel charges, and tolls. I was committed and dedicated. I knew God was peeling me, increasing my life flow. It was this evolutionary impulse that pulled me to be more. Oh yeah, it cost me my marriage and most of my salary, but the hero's journey is not about gaining or winning, it is about losing everything to be resurrected. My journey was in the best hands — God's. I surrendered. I was afraid, but I offered myself to love and transformation.

One day, as I sat on the foot of my hotel bed after a long duty day, I clicked the remote to turn on the TV. It was tuned to the PBS channel. The acclaimed journalist Bill Moyer was interviewing an older gentleman I didn't recognize. Intuitively my body opened and softened as his words on mythology and spirituality struck me like a lightning bolt — awakening me to a different realm and dimension. It was a new kind of truth, that shifting thing again. This wise mythology professor and author, Joseph Campbell, echoed some stories I had heard only months before with Dr. Estés's book, *Women Who Run with Wolves*.

I sat mesmerized by his storytelling. The words snatched a few layers off my psycho-emotional self and exposed a truth of metaphor and mythology regarding religion that I had not heard or known before. I sat open to experience a depth of my Soul that had been in the shadow of my mind. My mouth gaped as my heart swelled. I felt light. I was coming out of the darkness as I relinquished and abandoned the thoughts and ideas that no longer served me.

That PBS special program, which still runs today, is called *The Power of Myth*. I watched, riveted. When the PBS host asked for programming support of the station and offered a full three-DVD set of the series for $100, I dialed that 1-800 number without hesitation. It was crazy; I recalled having just bought a cool pink bumper sticker that read "Follow Your Bliss" a week or so before that I had placed on my vanity.

"Follow your bliss and the universe will open doors for you where there were only walls," Mr. Campbell said. I discovered my bliss, my passion, my journey, my Soul purpose, and I could name it — to simply "live for love." I finally got it.

My manifesto was crystal clear: Live4Love! There, she was born, in seven lucky characters . . . Liv4Lov. And when I bought my indigo (third eye) VW New Beetle with turbo manual transmission, with a Liv4Lov custom license plate, I decided that I would literally have a purposeful driven life. I love the bumper sticker and quote by Laurel Thatcher Ulrich, "Well-behaved women seldom make history." So drive on, sista wild woman!

I remember being coached by my older brother Michael that if you learn how to drive a stick shift, you will always be able to drive anything. I took his instruction at fifteen years old and learned how to drive his first car, a white VW Beetle.

I've learned that driving a stick shift keeps you more engaged. Symbolically, in life we are shifting through the sacred seven once again — gears 1, 2, 3, 4, 5, Neutral, and Reverse. And thank you God for REVERSE, a position when we just need to back up from a place we chose consciously or even unconsciously. We can throw that baby in Reverse when we make a wrong turn, a hasty decision, or wind up at the wrong location. We can quickly change course and begin again. We can begin at first gear and then keep it moving through the shifting of other gears until we can somewhat relax and cruise to fifth gear like on a straightaway or an open highway. We shift up through the gears to eventually go back down to second and stop in neutral. In neutral you pause, to begin again. There really are only two choices from neutral to get the car moving, and that is first gear or reverse. A driver can't start in the third, fourth, or fifth gears, and if attempting to start in second gear, the car will putter and stutter until it shifts to first gear again.

Our lives, when shifting through the consciousness of our awareness, are metaphorically like handling a manual transmission. We have all the gears to move forward and we must use them or we stagnate, putter, stutter and get stuck. We have our chakras, our wheels of light, the vibrating rainbow that illuminates the passage to higher consciousness and growth, emotionally, physically, and spiritually. We all must shift.

Driving an automatic car does have its benefits, such as driving and eating with one hand, because you have more freedom with your hands. Not that you can't drive and eat a burrito with a stick shift, it's just kind of awkward and flirts with the risk for a colossal mess. Trust me, there is nothing like having pieces of tortilla, cheesy beans, and rice slide off the wrapper and onto the gear shaft and in between the seat and the console . . . eeeewwww gross!

But being and living on automatic, as opposed to driving an automatic, offers the worst risk. Living in what may be perceived as a safe comfort zone does not allow for grace and growth. Not only that, safe is an illusionary state of being because absolutely everything changes and evolves. The same safe street that was once the most expeditious route to your favorite neighborhood store will eventually have to get repaved and you'll have to take a detour that will guide you down a once-forbidden street off the beaten path that leads you exactly where you need to go. And then again, we always have reverse . . . Thank you, God!

In life, shift happens, discovery happens, and a celebration of the journey is always forward. We have to cross the hero's threshold. When we limit ourselves to what we can become and know, unfortunately prejudice, stereotypes, and all-out ignorance manifest. But if we consciously shift, shake things up a bit, take a risk or two in our lives and let the wolf be wild, it can stimulate our creative nature. We become inspired to live for love and perhaps howl at the moon!

W*hen the solution is simple, God is answering.*
Albert Einstein

My personal message is easy . . . I live for love. And so it is! And when people think my personal message is cheesy, cheeky, idealistic, Polly Anna-ish or whatever, I just smile and drive my VW Beetle happily. What do YOU live for? Can you live deep and tell the truth, even through an aching heart? Can you *increase* your life and deepen your faith? Can you be peeled to pieces to uncover something so powerful that you weep with joy? Believe in your authentic power . . . strip fear away and snatch it from its grip.

Ｗ*e must be willing to get rid of the life we've planned, so as to have the life that is waiting for us. The old skin has to be shed before the new one can come.*

Joseph Campbell

The telling of stories, parables, and myths as well as some lies run deep within our human fabric. We weave stories to rationalize our fears so we won't have to tell the truth. Who are you if you never speak from your heart? Your Soul? How can one live? How have we lived with such lies for centuries?

The metaphysical *The Power of Now* and *A New Earth* author Eckhart Tolle says that we are living in a "collective drama" on this planet and until we awaken we will continue to say and do things that will NOT evolve us. We have serious issues that we must deal with and resolve, from race, ethnicity, and gender to politics and economics. The 2008 presidential election had too many issues that were primarily about race. President Barack Obama and his family, like no other candidate, had to deal with and continue to experience the most egregious slurs because of the color of their skin. Hollywood and its reality shows are out of control, and there are too many unpronounceable ingredients in our food. Our government lies, as we all have at some point, but their lies have been unspeakable and unfathomable. The truth of life cuts to the core, and many people just do not want to hear it. They would rather "spin it," play "pretend it never happened," and just hope their illusion will eventually be the truth. The blind lead the blind.

S ometimes letting things go is an act of far greater power than defending or hanging on.

Eckhart Tolle

What is the Truth? Works that have been interpreted literally, such as the Bible, perhaps are metaphors, parables, myths, and ideas that were told to inspire our very own glory and grace from God within. I believe Heaven resides IN us; it is not something OUT there to fulfill us, but it is what we have living inside us that already exists. We must not fall prey to things that divide us or allow us to be parasites. We are one nation under God wherever we live on this planet. Whether it is America or Iraq, we must accept and manifest more love and cultivate our spirits to bring hope, change, and peace to the world.

I was introduced to Yoruba, an African religion, during the "Follow Your Bliss" period in my life, which I call pre-9/11-2001. Now, the Yoruba people of West Africa, who live in Nigeria and Benin, have practiced a tradition of nature worship and ancestor reverence for thousands of years. The Yoruba worship one god, named Olodumare, along with dozens of deities known as orishas who are personified aspects of nature and spirit. The principal orishas include Eleggua, Oggun, Ochosi, Obatala, Yemaya, Oshun, and Shango. After my Mayan visit, back in Florida, a Yoruba priest named Baba Ona threw cowrie shells like dice to foretell my destiny and determine which orisha was my personification. My spirit is Yemaya. It is said that Yemaya is the great mother goddess of Santeria, the maternal force of life and creation. She is said to be the mother of many other orishas, and is believed to live in the ocean. She has many aspects, one of them as a fierce warrior.

The cowrie reading was a series of hand-tossed shakes with about seven cowries thrown on a special sacred mat. He said positive things about my spirit, which I resonated with and believed and knew to be true. He told me that my family and friends loved me dearly and that my life would be of service. He also said that I had some negative spirits or "haters" in my life who were trying to take away my joy. I was at a crossroads and needed to make a decision. His blessing for me to clear this energy was to kill a chicken and spread its blood on the tires of my vehicle. My hero's test was to drive to an intersection with the sacked bloody carcass, say the protective prayer he gave me, and place the dead chicken as close as I could to the center of the intersection — the crossroads — without getting caught.

I mean, how could I explain inhumane animal slaughter, trespassing, and littering to the police? They would have sent me straight to jail. But I was anxious about my life. I felt like I had a thousand monkeys in my head playing some silly tune and doing backflips. To be set free, I was determined to dispose of the bloody carcass at the perfect dark intersection and drive off like a bat outta hell as if I had done nothing wrong. So I drove from the Yoruba family's secluded home, never to see them again, and made my way to the crossroads to release my monkey mind, the dead chicken, and said my prayer of gratitude for spiritual healing and protection and drove away with quickness. I didn't look back.

Stand at the crossroads and look; ask for the ancient paths, ask where the good way is, and walk in it, and you will find rest for your souls.

Jeremiah 6:16

Even though my husband knew nothing of my chicken ordeal, it was clear when he told me that he thought I was "worshipping the devil" that this man did not know me from Eve. I was lost as to how to explain my path and what I had experienced or been experiencing. I asked him, "As much as I talk about love and God, and after naming my car LIV4LOV — why didn't you just talk to me?" He said "he was praying for me," as if I would snap out of my bliss. Frustrated, disappointed, and confused, I knew my marriage was completely over. I couldn't live in any more lies; to myself, my husband, my family, or anyone for that matter. I'd rather be single, a wild woman following her bliss, than living some half-truth feeling disconnected and misunderstood at a Soul level.

My journey's reward and gift from the call to adventure with the varied tests was that I became my own hero; I transformed and discovered the force within to carry on.

A hero, a shero, a warrior, a goddess, or a person who is committed to being an agent of change must have courage. I had to leap and step out on faith so the safety net could appear. God needs us to act from a place that is empty so he can bless us with his will. We must surrender. Joseph Campbell wrote, "The modern hero, the modern individual who dares to heed the call and seek the mansion of that presence with whom it is our whole destiny to be atoned cannot, indeed, must not, wait for his community to cast off its slough of pride, fear, rationalized avarice, and sanctified misunderstanding."

The philosopher Nietzsche said, "Live as though the day were here. It is not society that is to guide and save the creative hero, but precisely the reverse. Every one of us shares the supreme ordeal — carries the cross of the redeemer — not in the bright moments of his tribe's great victories, but in the silences of his personal despair."

It takes courage to grow up and turn out to be who you really are.

E. E. Cummings

Therefore, we must deepen our faith as a hero as never before. In yoga we deepen our postures and our breath. This is best illustrated in the pose Downward-Facing Dog, which to some yogis is the most dynamic asana or, as Baron Baptiste has said in his book *Journey into Power,* the "quintessential power yoga pose in that it engages your whole being." So much is going on in this posture. As your body moves into the posture, you lift the sitting bones and your butt into an inverted V as you simultaneously press the hills of your feet closer to reach the yoga mat, the earth, pushing down through strong open arms. Backs of legs outwardly rotating and pressing back; pressing forward on your mat by spreading your palms and keeping your fingers parallel. Your spine lengthens as your hamstrings release and melt with the pelvic tilt. This doggie-style posture is no joke. Your shoulders and wrists are strong in the pose, but the lift and power is in your core, the *Uddiyanha Bandha,* which is held firm by your "paws," the index finger and palms. Your shoulder blades slide back, an open relaxed neck and chest work toward the top of your thighs, and you can gaze past your ankles into "the abyss." You breathe deep — *Ujjayi* — effortlessly, victoriously lengthening your body, as you are free to float into the next posture. Yoga float: yoga flow. Joseph Campbell wrote, "It is by going down into the abyss that we recover the treasures of life. Where you stumble, there lies your treasure." And as you gaze out from your Downward Dog and into the abyss, the depths of its full expression surrender into the bliss of honoring the treasure, the gift of the "hero" — *Virasana!*

The adventure of the hero is the adventure of being alive.
Joseph Campbell

Nia (Swahili for "Purpose"): *To make our collective vocation the building and developing of our community in order to restore our people to their traditional greatness*

143

A

AWAKEN, Awareness, ACTIVISM

Warrior One/Won (Virabhadrasana I)

Sixth or Brow Chakra (Ajna)

Location	Center of the forehead
Color	Indigo-purple
Element	Light or mind, the higher expression of all signs
Sense	All senses
Sound	Re
Functions	Vision; the center of psychic power, higher intuition, the energies of the spirit, magnetic forces, and light, healing addictions, vitalizing the lower brain and central nervous system
Glands or organs	Pituitary gland, left eye, nose, ears, central nervous system
Qualities & lessons	Soul realization, insight, imagination, higher consciousness, emotional and spiritual love center, spiritual inner sight, clairvoyance, concentration, peace of mind, wisdom, devotion, imagination
Negative qualities	Fear, cynicism, headaches, eye problems, bad dreams, detachment, worry, hysteria, stress, fear, irritation, speech and weight problems
Gemstones	Lapis lazuli, amethyst, sapphire, iolite, moonstone

Ashtanga Path
Dharana (Concentration)

Army Core Value
Integrity

$\mathcal{S}ix$
AWAKEN, AWARENESS, ACTIVISM

Awakening is not a thing. It is not a goal, not a concept. It is not something to be attained. It is a metamorphosis. If the caterpillar thinks about the butterfly it is to become, saying 'And then I shall have wings and antennae,' there will never be a butterfly. The caterpillar must accept its own disappearance in its transformation. When the marvelous butterfly takes wing, nothing of the caterpillar remains.

Alejandro Jodorowsky

Andi was the pretty petite blonde who always migrated to the rear, far left-hand corner of my yoga class. She had always been the first one to arrive, looking rather pale and exhausted. She was quiet, but I knew there was more haunting her. We made small talk a few times about what we were doing in the Green Zone. She was an activist with the National Democratic Institute based in Washington, D.C., working to help Iraqi political

parties reach out to voters. Her job was more dangerous than mine, because she frequently went to the Red
Zone. The color was appropriate because during that
time in Baghdad, in 2006, the area was a blood bath.

B.A.G.H.D.A.D. Yoga was growing in popularity. It
was the place to get your mind right, work out, sweat,
and chill out with an OMMMM or two. I told Andi that
I designed a logo for T-shirts that I would sell and give
the proceeds to local Iraqi women and to the Women
for Women International nonprofit organization. The
T-shirt logo was a combination of the yin and yang
symbol, with the AUM symbol in the middle and the
words "B.A.G.H.D.A.D. Yoga" circling the sphere. It
was the perfect design for balance and peace. On the
back of the shirt were the words "B.A.G.H.D.A.D. Yoga"
and the blessing of Gandhi's quote "Be the change
you want to see."

Andi told me that she would support the effort, so
when the shirts arrived, she was the very first con-
tributor at ten dollars for each shirt. She selected an
olive-green T-shirt. Spontaneously, I suggested that we
take pictures so I could create a website to share our
story of peace through yoga in war-torn Baghdad. We
took pictures inside and outside of class with our hands
pressed together in the sacred prayer hand position,
anjali mudra. We also took a picture with our backs
together, casually sitting on the edge of the Liberty
Pool with big, cheesy grins, as if we were longtime
girlfriends and had been lounging outside or shopping
at the mall.

The dark background of the beautifully lit pool was actually a shadow of the grim reaper. We had not just finished shopping that day or been kicking back chillin' with mojitos or frothy piña coladas; we had miraculously survived another day, so our smiles were of genuine gratitude. We took a few more pictures with one of Andi's colleagues and with another Soldier, Staff Sergeant Ragin, whom I affectionately called "Grasshopper" because he was a devoted student who learned my yoga sequence and in a pinch would substitute teach for me. Though we hadn't had any cocktails that evening, we toasted our bodies during class and celebrated B.A.G.H.D.A.D. Yoga and the T-shirt design. We prayed that Gandhi's message of change on our shirts would be seen and felt in the shadow of the world and light it with our wish: the wish to change the threat of death for anyone who traveled to the Red Zone.

But that wish of change didn't happen in time. An ambush struck Andi's convoy the following week, on January 17, 2007. I do not remember where I was when I heard the news, but even to this day thinking about it brings me to overwhelming tears, as it did then. My heart just sinks. Andrea Parhamovich, at twenty-eight years of age, had accepted her call as a change agent to help Iraqis "build the kind of national level political institutions that can help bridge the sectarian divide and improve Iraqi lives," as the National Democratic Institute announced. She was a young woman with great promise. Most heartbreaking, she was set to marry

Michael Hastings on Valentine's Day. He was a journalist and as his final "love letter" in 2008 published their life story, *I Lost My Love in Baghdad: A Modern War Story*.

Activism takes courage and great risk. To be socially and politically active, to stand up and take action for the rights of others, is risky. To stand up for people who are economically or socially oppressed, or denied civil rights because of their gender, race, orientation, language, or eye color . . . is courageous. Activists are gifts from God!

A small white candle was lit in Andi's honor and was placed in front of my yoga mat when we practiced that evening. All the yogis in my class had the most spirited practice ever as we moved gracefully and prayerfully with each breath and posture. We dedicated each movement to Andi's spirit. We asked in humble prayer for the continued protection of the angels — those at our right, left, behind, front, and below — those that are all around us to guide us and keep us safe in the Zone. We wiped tears and sealed our practice with a unified beautiful chorus of three Ommms. It was so loud with vibration; certainly heaven heard and felt our cries for peace.

Your vision will only become clear when you look into your heart. Who looks outside, dreams, Who looks inside, awakens.

Carl Jung

M. J. Abbitt, who wrote one of my "open letters" in this book, was a committed yogi and my biggest fan. She thanked me for a remarkable class. I thanked and hugged her for being there, too. Abbitt, a woman in her early fifties, also leads a life of activism. She had had major knee surgeries before arriving in country, but was rehabilitating them during my class. She was working with the United States Agency for International Development, whose core mission is to provide economic development and humanitarian assistance around the world in support of foreign policy goals. One might possibly look at her and instantly think she's a retired schoolteacher, not the feisty woman she actually is, working to educate and empower Iraqis. M. J. believes in change, she believes in hope, and she actively pursues opportunities that will reach the greater good. She inspires me.

As I mentioned before, my mother is also a testament to activism. At seventy-two years old, she decided to return to the workforce and was appointed the director of a senior activity center in Bakersfield, California. She single-handedly took a space where they played bingo once a week and served lunch, and turned it into to a thriving active center with educational workshops that ranged from diet and fitness to fashion. My mother replaced what was an unused plot of land and an eyesore with a flourishing atrium memory garden that has a sitting bench named in honor of a deceased visitor who too represented activism and service. My mom's twenty-hours-a-week gig was her mission to create change in the lives of other senior citizens. She saw an opening, an opportunity, and rose to the challenge with her eyes open, awake and ready to do the work.

Activism is born when we awaken to the fact that each of us has a powerful purpose on this planet. Though most people will manifest their purpose in a positive manner, others will choose darkness or lurk in the shadows in the gray areas, not showing up and not being accountable. You know the type. These sleepwalkers want you to do things for them. They want instant gratification with no effort or patience. They blame others for not achieving their desires. We all have a light to shine and to share. There is no age limit. Bad knees can't stop you. Being in Baghdad, at war, or in some remote African village or embedded deep within the Mayan rainforest does not absolve you from being the change you want to see in the world. Gandhi knew this, as did Dr. Martin Luther King Jr. and Mother Teresa. My wish is that when we die, we know that we took risks, removed the blindfolds, crawled out from under our rocks, acted courageously, and lived in the powerful fullness of a spiritual warrior. The spiritual warrior sees beyond the veil, into the truth. In his book *The Four Agreements*, don Miguel Ruiz defines the spiritual warrior as "a person who challenges the dreams of fear, lies, false beliefs, and judgments that create suffering and unhappiness in his or her life. It is a war that takes place in the heart and mind of a man or woman."

During my time as a spiritual albeit peaceful warrior and art-ivist in Baghdad, I was also fortunate to help facilitate that unconditional love on the other side of battle with a group of interested service members and civilians called HUB — Humanitarians United for Baghdad. This short-lived group consolidated its members' efforts to collect clothing, backpacks, wheelchairs, and whatever else activists from around the world sent to share with the Iraqis. My MNSTC-I health affairs office collected boxes from churches. Effective and efficient distribution was always the biggest obstacle because there was no safe way to do it. The schools in the Green Zone received the majority of the donations, while select schools and orphanages outside the zone were not as fortunate because they were harder to reach and in dangerous areas. Our rudimentary distribution plan was contacting known units that were conducting ground patrols and wanted to assist in our endeavors. We also had Colonel Hassan personally drop off the boxes full of goodies at local orphanages in the Red Zone. On occasion he brought us pictures of the children dressed in their new clothing and playing with their stuffed animals and toys.

One day I was able to assist other activists and official Boy Scout leaders supporting the Green Zone Council of Iraq Boy and Girl Scouts by cleaning up an abandoned plot of land, which was a park adjacent to Saddam's Baghdad Zoo. It was a long day of pure enjoyment and satisfaction. We hauled tree limbs and thick brush into large piles; we gathered debris of all sorts to uncover a field of possibility. We shared meals ready to eat (MREs). I delighted in teaching the young scouts about our American military delicacy: how to open the brown bag and heat the entrée without getting burned or dropping any portion of the contents in the dirt. We all cheered at the successful scouting mission, took pictures together, American and coalition service members, Iraqi women, men, boys and girls — together. Before we went our separate ways, a scout and I exchanged patches from our uniform; in that moment of possibility, of interconnectedness, there was nothing but pure love between us.

As I was set to redeploy back home in 2007, Violet, the Iraqi woman who worked with the Iraqi surgeon general, recognized me as a spiritual warrior in my own right by presenting me with a small carved plastic statue of Ishtar, the ancient Sumero-Babylonian goddess of love and fertility, a war goddess, also known as the lioness of the battle. Ishtar was a goddess of justice and healing . . . I thought that was super cool!

What is even cooler is the yoga posture *Virabhadrasana* or Warrior I (Warrior Won) . . . Warriors Win! This powerful posture integrates leg and hip strength. You take a step forward and lunge deeply, making your hips square while lifting your arms overhead, as if you are ready to duel the enemy of apathy, self-doubt, and ignorance.

I challenge everyone to wake up from the sleepy slumber of indifference and complacency, and embrace the battle to overcome any obstacle, which is really

FEAR — False Evidence Appearing Real. Slay your fears triumphantly! Change how you see: Change your "C" by simply moving your "sCared" to the "saCred." Be that spiritual gangster: a Warrior, NOT a wimpy, whiny Worrier! Take the journey of courage. As Lao Tzu says, "A journey of a thousand miles must begin with a single step." Take a deep breath and a giant lunge forward . . . exhale and leeeeeeeeaap. Believe me, the safety net will appear!

Kuumba (Swahili for "Creativity"): *To do always as much as we can, in the way we can, in order to leave our community more beautiful and beneficial than we inherited it*

D

DEATH of the EGO: Devotion, DESTINY, divinity

Lotus Pose (Padmasana)

Seventh or Crown Chakra (Sahasrara)

Location	Crown of the head
Color	Violet or white
Element	Thought/will/bliss; the higher expression of all elements
Sense	All senses including cosmic consciousness
Sound	Ti
Functions	Fulfillment; vitalizes the upper brain, the center of spirituality, enlightenment, dynamic thought and energy
Glands or organs	Pineal gland, cerebrum, central nervous system, right eye
Qualities & lessons	Unification of the Higher Self with the human personality, oneness with the Infinite, spiritual will, inspiration, unity, divine wisdom, idealism, selfless service, perception beyond space and time; the inward flow of wisdom from the ether and the gift of cosmic consciousness
Negative qualities	Lack of inspiration, confusion, depression, alienation, hesitation to serve, senility, confusion, anxiety, stress
Gemstones	Amethyst, diamond, clear quartz, white howlite, moonstone, purple fluorite, quartz crystal

Ashtanga Path
Dhyana (Meditation)

Army Core Value
Personal Courage

Seven

DEATH OF THE EGO, DEVOTION, DESTINY, DIVINITY

I believe in signs . . . what we need to learn is always there before us, we just have to look around us with respect & attention to discover where God is leading us and which step we should take. When we are on the right path, we follow the signs, and if we occasionally stumble, the Divine comes to our aid, preventing us from making mistakes.

Paulo Coelho

When we reach our purple "reign," our crown chakra, by having "wheeled" (willed) ourselves from our root chakra, through our pelvis, on up around our solar plexus, through our heart chakra and our throat, penetrating out of our third eye and finally glowing through our crown chakra of light, we are reaching through layers of emotions, mental and physical scars and wounds so deep and tears so big that at *Samadhi* ("enlightenment or self-actualization") healing occurs. The crown has been earned. We're frightened no more.

Prince is my favorite musical artist of ALL time. His masterpiece song is "Purple Rain"; in it he tells his listeners that we want a leader but "can't seem to make up your mind" so we need to be guided to the Purple Rain. This prodigy and genius was able to write, play, produce and *guide* his own music-work as a teenager, but there was a time when he was unable to guide and lead his work, and he literally changed into a sign, an unpronounceable symbol, which is a combination of the symbols for male (♂) and female (♀): the Love Symbol (⚥). I believe this change illustrated how he was breaking through to his authentic self — to his Divinity.

Initially a solo artist, Prince introduced his band, The Revolution, in 1984, and later created The New Power Generation in 1990. He was courageous, as he creatively transformed, evolved to become The Artist Formerly Known as Prince or TAFKAP for seven years, from 1993 to 2000.

TAFKAP also scrawled the word "slave" with an eyeliner pencil on the side of his cheek to protest the terms of his contract with Warner Bros. The "CON-tract" which he referred to, or as I love to say, "the golden handcuffs," that we may sometimes find ourselves in may be limiting our potential, thus enslaving us in ways that do not serve us. In one of his rare interviews, Prince stated, "I became merely a pawn used to produce more money for Warner Bros. . . . I was born Prince and did not want to adopt another conventional name. The only acceptable replacement for my name, and my identity, was the Love Symbol, a symbol with no pronunciation, that is a representation of me and what my music is about. This symbol is present in my work over the years; it is a concept that has evolved from my frustration; it is who I am. It is my name."

As TAFKAP, he was able to release several more albums than his contract would have allowed by the moniker Prince. I believe when you have divine inspiration, a song, or a calling, you must share this gift from our Creator. It is destiny. By manifesting the glory of the Creator, we are, in fact, in heaven.

Our gift is that thing which calls us forward, higher, and inspires us to do more, to be and to do what liberates us from bondage, whether self-imposed or imposed by others. Even if we have to change our name, divorce one, two, three times, relocate to four different states in two years, return to school, cut our hair, forgive someone, or just plain love unconditionally — change must happen. Above all, we must act in accordance with our Soul's purpose. Despite naysayers or folks who can't pronounce our name or understand our (il) logic, we all should/must eventually live authentically to know Heaven.

Prince, my beloved musical genius, TAFKAP, was doing just that — living authentically. Finally, in 1996, he was liberated from his contract and released a triple-CD concept album, *Emancipation*. Each twelve-song disc is exactly one hour in length. There is a lot of symbolism surrounding the album; the number of songs, discs, and each song's length has a connection to astrology and the Egyptian pyramids. Interestingly to me, of course, is Prince's fascination with numbers,

157

as seen is his video "3 Chains o' Gold," the song "7," and the CD and song "3121," just to name a few.

This leads me to believe that Prince, "the Royal Purple Badness," has studied numerology and the seven chakras. The highest chakra — the crown chakra or thousand-petaled lotus — is represented by the color violet or purple, his favorite color. And oh, by the way, Prince's 2009 release of another three-disc set was beautifully titled and spelled as *LOtUSFLOW3R*.

The color purple is also significant in the military. The Purple Heart is awarded to servicemen and -women for being wounded or even killed in combat; it is considered the most honorable medal given for an injury incurred in battle. This little ribbon that decorates the left side of recipients' chests symbolizes their lost parts: parts of their lives, of their minds, and of their bodies they can never replace. For some it graces their uniform and spirit, and for others it has been a disgrace as there have been Soldiers known for receiving the Purple Heart for cowardice . . . yes!

It is a sad, but true, fact that terrified Soldiers throughout history have been known to self-inflict nonlethal injuries so they can be medically evacuated to the rear, leaving their brothers in arms in jeopardy. Better yet, a few Soldiers aka "PX Rangers" will help themselves to an assortment of ribbons without being authorized, placing them on their uniform and declaring their gallantry and bravery. Forget God, duty, honor, country — they are all about "the ego."

The Stolen Valor Act of 2005 set out penalties for people who falsely claim to have been awarded the

Purple Heart. The act stated that any false verbal, written, or physical claim, or selling of the Purple Heart Medal by an individual to whom it has not been awarded is a federal offense punishable by jail time and/or a fine. In June 2012, the act was deemed to be unconstitutional and struck down because it violated our right to free speech. What? So there are fakers out there dressing up and impersonating wounded warriors and they haven't done a damn thang! What a shame.

What I know for sure is that we are to live our lives with integrity; we MUST be devoted to truth. We have the ability to unleash a strength and determination to set ourselves free in order to transform. It is our destiny, ultimately, just as the musician Prince transformed from a "slave" to a king. He earned his purple crown through an arduous journey to own his incredible music and to claim his name: his Soul and to be a great artistic Warrior. I believe it is what we all must do to rightfully reclaim what is ours to own.

We must do it with guts and grit to see through the fog of our personal "ego war" to find our truth. Now we may, at any given time, shrink in fear or we may hide in pain from any drama or dilemma we may experience, but we are called to stand up to harassment, intolerance, and prejudice of any kind. We must support our children in trouble and heal broken relationships.

Our deepest fear is not that we are inadequate. Our deepest fear is that we are powerful beyond measure. It is our light, not our darkness, that most frightens us. We ask ourselves, who am I to be brilliant,

22222222222

gorgeous, talented, fabulous? Actually, who are you *not* to be? You are a child of God. Your playing small doesn't serve the world. There's nothing enlightened about shrinking so that other people won't feel insecure around you. We are all meant to shine, as children do. We were born to make manifest the glory of God that is within us. It's not just in some of us; it's in everyone. And as we let our own light shine, we unconsciously give other people permission to do the same. As we're liberated from our own fear, our presence automatically liberates others.

Marianne Williamson

The execution of Saddam Hussein took place on December 30, 2006. He was sentenced to death by hanging after being found guilty and convicted of "crimes against humanity" by an Iraqi special tribunal. Saddam Hussein's trial had been going on for a few weeks before I learned about an opportunity to attend in late October. I don't remember all the requirements for those who were invited to the courthouse. I know as an observer I was required to wear civilian clothing — absolutely no uniforms were allowed — so I had to go to the PX to buy khaki pants and a polo-style shirt.

I loaded the tour bus with other nosey Saddam onlookers. I was really just flat-out nosey and curious about what he and his accomplices looked like. I had no real understanding of the courtroom etiquette or protocol, not to mention Iraqi standards. I had heard (from where I don't know) that sometimes Saddam would stand up and yell, and raise and pump his fist in the air against his inevitable death sentence for the crimes he allegedly committed. I admit I wanted to see some drama, as if being in Baghdad wasn't drama enough.

The most I knew about court proceedings was from the pathetic, drama-filled TV judge shows like *Judge Judy*, where the judge snarls and slams the gavel down on the ex-boyfriend for taking advantage of his baby mama and not paying his part of the $400 rent. I don't like those shows. Yes, I am judging. I especially do not care for the "Who's my baby daddy?" à la Maury Povich paternity test shows or *The Real Housewives of* . . . Yep, real drama. You have to ask yourself, "Are these people FOR REAL?"

So I wanted to see Saddam, the martyr, the legend, and see if he was REAL. I was excited. No weapons were allowed in the courtroom, so I left my sidekick firearm behind. I felt odd and suddenly naked, vulnerable, even awkward. Good thing I had my camera; though I was instructed not to use it to take pictures, I surely could throw it at someone's head if need be and if things got funky in the courthouse. I tucked my camera safely away in my back pocket, just in case.

I wasn't sure what type of drama showdown I would experience because I didn't exactly know the crimes Saddam and his homies supposedly committed or what weapons of mass destruction he had allegedly amassed. I really was open for anything; I was nosey.

A group of about twenty or so other nosey people were escorted to a seating area that was like box seats above a theater stage but completely enclosed in glass.

We were instructed to use headphones that plugged into a transistor radio. I looked out the glass to the pit of the courthouse below. Straight ahead was the judge and on both sides of him were people who I assumed were Iraqi jurors. Directly below our box seats sat Saddam and his boys. Saddam's first cousin, Ali Hassan al-Majid, formerly known as "Chemical Ali," wore the traditional white sheik's robe called a djellaba and headdress with a black headband called a kaffiyeh. Others, like Saddam, wore Western-style business suits. He looked tired, they all did. I couldn't believe what I was hearing as I listened to a witness who was strategically placed behind a black curtain and detailed a horrific event that Saddam's regime had committed.

The language translations in the courtroom went from Kurdish to Arabic to English. My mind was fried after trying to follow the story line and then the questions and subsequent answers with the same translation process back and forth. I couldn't pay attention that long. At some point I just wanted Saddam to stand up, shake his fist, yell profanities, and proclaim "I DID NOT have sex with THAT woman!" or something. There were too many languages at once, fast and then slow. Eventually, I removed my headphones and found an old newspaper to read. I looked up every now and again to see if Saddam had a dramatic outburst or public meltdown.

The fact is, this trial was NOT exciting to me. I was a nosey spectator watching a man about to be sentenced to death for doing only God knows what. I wanted to leave, but the show wasn't over yet and the group had to leave together. Instead of wanting to see Saddam act rebellious, I finally came to my senses and prayed. I prayed for understanding, forgiveness, and justice. Not only did I pray for the hidden and frightened witness speaking Kurdish through tears behind the black curtains, but for Saddam, his boys, and all the nosey people watching. I prayed that when we are in the trials of our lives we can tell our truth and admit the crime we committed, atone, and shift back to joy, integrity, and selflessness. I prayed that we could do this and we could also stand up for what is right. I prayed that we could say, "I AM my brother's keeper, what I do to YOU returns to ME. May I act honorably and may WE live in a world that works for everyone."

Though we may have only glimpses at times of what enlightenment may look like, it is really when we trust and allow what it is to be — just be. When we are free from the chains of slavery that may have held us captive to our internal self-bondage, we will then no longer be cellmates but Soul mates on this planet, and we will truly be able to evolve in our Divinity.

B reak yourself free from your hereditary patterns, cultural codes, social beliefs; and prove once and for all that the power within you is greater than the power that's in the world.
Dr. Michael Bernard Beckwith

My last yoga class in Baghdad was an energetic and somber one. We laughed and moved with strength and power. My Australian down-under yogis would yell "THUNDER" in their Aussie accents when we moved to Thunderbolt (*Utkatasana*). We'd giggle as we raised our arms overhead while squatting our hips in a difficult air chair position, concentrating on the movement and our breath.

In our last class, we moved through our *Vinyasa* with true unconditional love and connection. We rinsed and wringed out the toxins from of our bodies, peeled the onion, and used every other surrendering metaphor that would take us to our final resting posture, so we could chill out, let go, and breathe. I played some slow melodic music that would reverberate off our sweaty skin. We laid supine, arms limply on sides of body with palms up, eyes closed, stilling our breath and calming our hearts.

In yoga, the Corpse Pose (*Savasana*) is the final pose in nearly all practices. I call it the "OK, now chill out and let it ALL go" pose because, well, "Corpse" Pose just didn't quite encourage the yogis in my class. Corpse was not cool! Resting in *Savasana* peace allows the body and breath to recover and restore from an invigorating yoga practice. After a good musical piece of about five to ten minutes, we did a final stretch and lay on our sides in the fetal position with eyes closed before coming to the final sitting posture — Lotus. With our hands pressed together in prayer, we sealed the practice with one resounding deep AUM in unison. We pressed our thumb knuckles to the middle of our foreheads, our third eye, the seat of our spiritual intuitive center, bowed, and said, "Namaste." We were restored and transformed to live and pray for another day.

I vowed during that last class in Baghdad that B.A.G.H.D.A.D. Yoga would live on. I would tell my story and continue to teach anywhere I went to promote yoga as a means of actualizing health and peace of mind — specifically for my brothers and sisters in arms.

War takes its toll on Soldiers, airmen, marines, sailors, and civilians as well as governments, nations, and local neighborhoods. It wreaks havoc on families and can ruin relationships. It is only through committed and compassionate living that we may rise above the pettiness and disdain that we may have for our fellow man. We must triumph as Warriors, slay the beasts, the mental dragons of hate and fear, and become heroes and stand for what is fair and just. We must believe in goodness. We must be the change as miracle workers.

Possibly you've been lost before and you found a kiosk with a map that read *You Are Here.* Where you are at the time determines how close you are to your final destination. Well, somehow, you are HERE in nearly the last paragraph of *B.A.G.H.D.A.D. Yoga,* and you either read the book in its entirety or just skipped around. Either way, you are HERE and this journey I shared with you has at minimum seven basic takeaway ideas I'd wish for you to experience or remember for your ongoing personal journey:

1. We must BREATHE and fight the good fight; We must BE it. Be about it. Believe it, and count every single Blessing. We must strive for Balance in every Breath we take.
2. We must be a change Agent with the ATTITUDE and Awareness that we are the ones we have been waiting for — AWESOME!

3. We must Grow Goodness with Gratitude and thank God for her GRACE because with anything less we will not have a planet to live on.

4. We absolutely must HEAL our Hearts and choose to live in Harmony as it is in Heaven. YOU are the Hero; don't worry, be Happy!

5. We must DEEPEN our Faith and have the Discipline and Dignity to do what we must do to . . .

6. AWAKEN and take Action and Answer the call to service as an Activist and serve honorably.

7. We are powerful beyond measure; therefore we must work towards the Death of the ego and rise like a phoenix from its ashes, spreading its transformative wings for our DIVINITY. It is our Destiny; it is the B.A.G.H.D.A.D. Yoga journey wishing YOU to Devote yourself to being the change in the world!

Thank you . . . OK now . . . ALL together . . . inhale, exhale . . . Ommmm . . . Namaste!

We must return our charges — our children and our veterans, our deeds and our dreams, our soldiers and our adversaries — to the path of the mystic warrior. And we must do so in the name of healing, reconciliation, and restoration. We must make the pursuit of peace as mythic as the pursuit of war has been. The fate of our world depends upon how successfully we undertake and carry through this great task.

Edward Tick

Samadhi (Enlightenment): *This is the ultimate goal of the Eight Limbs of Yoga. It is characterized by the state of ecstasy and the feeling that you and the universe are one. It is a state of peace and completion, awareness and compassion with detachment.*

Imani (Swahili for "Faith"): *To believe with all our heart in our people, our parents, our teachers, our leaders and the righteousness and victory of our struggle*

Live 4 Love

Love is patient, love is kind. It does not envy, it does not boast, it is not proud. It is not rude, it is not self-seeking, it is not easily angered, it keeps no record of wrongs. Love does not delight in evil but rejoices with the truth. It always protects, always trusts, always hopes, always perseveres . . . Love never fails. But where there are prophecies, they will cease; where there are tongues, they will be stilled; where there is knowledge, it will pass away. For we know in part and we prophesy in part, but when perfection comes, the imperfect disappears. When I was a child, I talked like a child, I thought like a child, I reasoned like a child. When I became a man, I put childish ways behind me . . . And now these three remain: faith, hope, and love. But the greatest of these is love.

1 Corinthians 13

The Soldier's Creed

Incorporating
THE WARRIOR ETHOS

I am an American Soldier.

I am a Warrior and a member of a team.

I serve the people of the United States and live the Army Values.

I will always place the mission first.

I will never accept defeat.

I will never quit.

I will never leave a fallen comrade.

I am disciplined, physically and mentally tough, trained and proficient in my warrior tasks and drills.

I always maintain my arms, my equipment, and myself.

I am an expert and I am a professional.

I stand ready to deploy, engage, and destroy the enemies of the United States of America in close combat.

I am a guardian of freedom and the American way of life.

I am an American Soldier.

Open Letters

A LETTER TO MICKEY

by M. J. Abbitt, a civilian U.S. citizen who worked in Iraq

Every Tuesday, Thursday, and Saturday evening I gathered with many others inside the International Zone's Recreation Center near the U.S. embassy to attend your yoga classes. Those evenings highlighted my days working for USAID (United States Agency for International Development) with Baghdad's new democratically elected members of its Provincial Council. I was seldom able to attend all three weekly practices as decision makers inside the IZ's walled compound — an assortment of trailers we called "home," located on the banks of the Tigris River next to the animal manager's house where Uday Hussein kept his personal zoo — forbid me to walk outside the gate. To go, I had to find a ride — difficult, often impossible — especially on days where we expected or experienced "incoming." Still, today I instinctively pattern my personal yoga on your poses and instructions; they leave me more relaxed and confident in mind, body, and spirit:

"Sun Salutation — Inhale. Grind to the heels, sweep up to the high, look up. Release, exhale."

"Forward standing bend — rag doll — bobblehead."

"Upward-Facing Dog — Shine Your Heart."

"Happy Baby — Slowly roll up and grab your feet with each hand and rock back and forth."

"Down Dog — Now walk your dog."

"Go at your own pace," you said as we began lying on mats, giving both newcomers and experienced yogis increased confidence. Room floor space was always full so we practiced positions, literally mat-to-mat, with feet or arms touching or crossing as each attempted their poses. "All good," you said, always with a smile on your face and in your voice which we both saw and heard as — breathing, stretching, moving — we looked up. Usually more men than women attended — body armor and weapons of both sexes stacked carefully along walls with weights and exercise equipment. Yoga students changed constantly as short- and long-term military and civilians deployed in and out of Baghdad. That was good, as we made many new friends.

On January 17, 2007, tragedy stuck. Andi Parham-ovich, the twenty-eight-year-old public communications specialist with the National Democratic Institute was killed in Baghdad, along with her security detail. They were returning to the IZ in convoy after training local NGO leaders in democracy awareness and development. Andi practiced her yoga on a mat lying in the center back of our rectangular room; she was no longer there. You lit a candle that evening, and we dedicated the class to Andi. Your lessons were strong, positive and dynamic, yet I remember this evening as quiet, thoughtful and thankful — as we all said good by to Andi. At session's close your words — "Angels to the front of us . . . to the back of us . . . to our right and left . . . under and over us . . . guide and protect us" — left each person quiet and unusually appreciative of our own person, meaning, and place. That evening we saw Andi (her young smile and spirit) as we sent our thanks, thoughts, and prayers to her — and to her parents, far away in Ohio.

I lost other friends — Iraqis — in my twelve months on the ground: Fatima, a strong yet tactful lady NGO leader who initiated a well-respected campaign to clean up the Tigris River and security guards — all killed violently as they went about the business of rebuilding their country and their lives. Many daily happenings also challenged me: my office window was located high above the Ibn Sina Hospital Emergency Room door, overlooking the runway where helicopters landed 24/7 to hurriedly carry in wounded warriors on litters for medical care — and those in body bags who did not make it. Too many afternoons I watched as vast plumes of black smoke spiraled high above Baghdad when suicide bombers struck — killing women and children just home from school shopping in local markets for their family's evening meal. A more helpless feeling I had never experienced. B.A.G.H.D.A.D. Yoga classes gave me leave to sleep at night, and make some sort of peace with these tragic happenings of war.

Working with USAID since 1998, I have been privileged to visit over a dozen countries around the globe, providing governance and development guidance for emerging markets, the countries' leaders, and citizens. I studied and learned various ways to focus mentally and physically: 1998 in Kazakhstan practicing Russian mat gymnastics with Natasha; on the evening of 9/11 crying nearly uncontrollably to myself in a Podgorica, Montenegro, aerobics class; Bulgaria in 2004 where Maria shared with me her favorite yoga asana, "reclining hand to toe," also declaring it to be "Madonna's favorite pose"; Romanian Natalia, voted the 2004 European International Aerobics Instructor Champion, who shared with me her best post-exercise breathing close, a modified Sun Sequence stretch; and in Indonesia a hotel Pilates teacher continually reminded me to "hold in my tummy!"

None match the peace and confidence your Baghdad yoga classes gave me.

A WOMAN'S EXPERIENCE

by Wassan Alber, a citizen of Iraq

My name is Wassan Alber, nicknamed "Violet." I'm a Catholic living in Baghdad, the land of continuous war violence from 1974, my year of birth, till now.

I like to share my experience for every talented, powerful lady which can give her all to help or to mix into her friends' spirits. I was growing up at Baghdad and when I became a teenager I went with my family to Sudan, Al Khartum (Africa), where I lived for three years. There I got involved with Moslems, Christians, girls from south to north of Africa. I was spreading love, sympathy, between all. I began to ask myself many questions. At my home, Sudan, there is much of poverty, diseases like AIDS, but I still am the girl that can give a hand for all girls around, taking strength from the Holy Spirit.

And I can communicate with all kinds of woman from all religions and cultures. Then after three years I had the chance to stay in Brasília, Brazil, for three years more. I become same and much more, when there was freedom, no violence, but women, girls, teenagers suffering from raping every night at Brazil. I was watching carefully new cases of rape, violence of married, divorced. Returning to my country [as it was] entering a new war, but this war was to liberate us from what we had become under Saddam's regime. After the war, 2003, we have many rights. We can make consider-able and vital decisions in our lives and our society in general. We are becoming more aware and independent every day. This awareness makes us more sensitive to other women's difficulties and the problems that are increasing day by day. Meanwhile I was married and have two kids, a daughter & son. I have a beautiful family with a engineering husband so I decided to make challenge. Responsibilities are loaded on me, but all that gives me a push to respect what I'm in by getting much experience. I decided to work to earn my living. In Iraq I met many U.S.A. military ladies. I worked as a translator. On the other hand I felt content when I saw uneducated women running their houses and their small business perfectly under bombs and explosions and poverty, raping, kidnapping. Such things [as the women's endurance] affect my life positively & make me feel how strong and talented woman are at all communities where I have lived. Every lady I met considers me as an open-minded woman who respects the difference between us all, but I seize every depressed upset weak lady, transmitting the whole strength spirit that shines from God through nature.

DARKNESS TO THE LIGHT

by Master Sergeant Reginald McMillian, Operation Enduring Freedom 2009–2010

I am not too sure just where to begin with all of this. I have been honestly searching for the place where, like Alice, I too fell down the rabbit hole. I am walking through that region of myself, which I have tried to avoid. Although I did not want to be there, I found myself pulled back there like one of those episodes of *The Twilight Zone* where no matter how many times you try to escape . . . you reenter the same room. They call this PTSD; the rest of life seems normal but you are different somehow.

I was different after returning from theater, but I thought that my difference was normal different. I never once considered the fact that my normal was not normal. After all I am a medic, and therefore, I should be able to tell if there is something wrong with me or not . . . right? After all I passed all of the post deployment evaluations; I just told them what I thought they wanted to hear . . . that I was a GO. But I have not slept through a entire night since I returned home. Some nights I sit up watching my wife sleep and thinking about what I would do if someone broke into our home.

So I started yoga after much prompting. Immediately the first problem I experienced was reconnecting with my body. I did not want to be mindfully present, what I wanted was to be somewhere else . . . anywhere else but present. It can be very difficult to stay in your own body when you're getting flashbacks. The lighting changes, and you feel like you're not even in the room. My flashbacks come with little warning and can be triggered by anything that reminds of what I am trying to forget. However, I am learning to relax better and sleep throughout the night. My wife says that I toss and turn less since I started my "mindfulness experience."

Yoga reminds me that if I just keep plodding along, I can get there. I can face it in little chunks; I can take one step at a time. I am learning how to face a past which still terrifies me. But I do it little by little. I have my own personal demons to face and with the help of my teachers/advisors I am doing just that. I can understand why some trauma survivors initially find yoga threatening. It is scarier for me to discover my body than to take a pill.

Most of the positions still hurt to get into because of my back, shoulders, and knees, but I do what I can. I can see now what I could not see before, in others and myself. And I have gained a mental clarity which, frankly, I am still uncomfortable with. I am on the right path to living with PTSD. But there are others who continue to "suck it up." For them The War continues without end.

Glossary

MILITARY TERMS

ACU: Army Combat Uniform
BDE: Brigade
BIAP: Baghdad International Airport
BN: Battalion
CDR: Commander
COL: Colonel
CPT: Captain
DFAC: Dining Facility
DIV: Division
FOB: Forward Operating Bases
IED: Improvised Explosive Device
LBE: Load Bearing Equipment
LTC: Lieutenant Colonel
MNSTC-I: Multi-National Security Training Command–
    Iraq
MRE: Meals Ready to Eat
NCO: Noncommissioned Officer
PT: Physical Training
PX: Post Exchange
ROE: Rules of Engagement
ROTC: Reserve Officer Training Corps
R&R: Rest and Relaxation
RTD: Return to Duty
SGO: (Iraqi) Surgeon General's Office
WTU: Warrior Transition Unit
XO: Executive Officer

YOGA POSTURES (ASANAS) MENTIONED

 Standing at Attention (*Samasthiti*)

 Mountain Pose (*Tadasana*)

 Standing Forward Bend (*Uttanasana*)

 Low Push-up (*Chaturanga Dandasana*)

 Child's Pose (*Balasana*)

 Cobra (*Bhujangasana*)

 Upward-Facing Dog (*Urdhva Mukha Svanasana*)

 Crow (*Bakansa*)

 Downward-Facing Dog (*Adho Muka Svanasana*)

 Warrior One/Won (*Virabhadrasana I*)

 Corpse Pose (*Savasana*)

 Lotus Pose (*Padmasana*)

 Hero (*Virasana*)

182

THE SEVEN MAJOR CHAKRAS

 The Crown Chakra (*Sahasrara*)

 The Brow Chakra (*Ajna*)

 The Throat Chakra (*Vishuddha*)

 The Heart Chakra (*Anahata*)

 The Solar Plexus Chakra (*Manipura*)

 The Sacral Chakra (*Svadisthana*)

 The Root Chakra (*Muladhara*)

ASHTANGA: THE EIGHTFOLD PATH, OR THE EIGHT LIMBS OF YOGA

Yama: Universal morality, ethical disciplines
Niyama: Personal observances, self-observation
Asanas: Body postures
Pranayama: Breathing exercises and control of *prana*
Pratyahara: Control of the senses, sense withdrawal
Dharana: Concentration and cultivating inner perceptual awareness
Dhyana: Devotion, meditation on the Divine
Samadhi: Union with the Divine, a state of joy and peace

Yama

The first limb, *yama*, deals with one's ethical standards and sense of integrity, focusing on our behavior and how we conduct ourselves in life. *Yamas* are universal practices that relate best to what we know as the Golden Rule, "Do unto others as you would have them do unto you." The five *yamas* are:

> *Ahimsa* (nonviolence, nonharming)
> *Satya* (truthfulness)
> *Asteya* (nonstealing)
> *Brahmacharya* (continence)
> *Aparigraha* (noncovetousness)

Niyama

Niyama, the second limb, has to do with self-discipline and spiritual observances. Regularly attending temple or church services, saying grace before meals, developing your own personal meditation practices, or making a habit of taking contemplative walks alone are all examples of *niyamas* in practice. The five *Niyamas* are:

> *Saucha* (cleanliness)
>
> *Samtosa* (contentment)
>
> *Tapas* (heat; spiritual austerities)
>
> *Svadhyaya* (study of the sacred scriptures and of oneself)
>
> *Isvara pranidhana* (surrender to God)

ARABIC WORDS AND PHRASES

habibi (male), *habibati* (female) or *habibti* (female colloquial): my beloved; also used for friend, darling, and similar endearments

marhaba: hello

inshallah: if Allah wills; God willing

shukran: thank you

hijab: A head covering or scarf worn by Muslim women

hib: love

assalamu alaikum: peace be upon you

Bibliography

This bibliography indicates the reading which has formed my ideas. I offer it as a guide for your journey.

Arewa, Caroline Shola. *Opening to Spirit : Contacting the Healing Power of the Chakras and Honouring African Spirituality.* London: Thorsons, 1998.

Armstrong, Keith, Suzanne Best, and Paula Domenici. *Courage After Fire: Coping Strategies for Troops Returning from Iraq and Afghanistan and Their Familes.* Berkeley: Ulysses Press, 2006.

Campbell, Joseph. *The Hero with a Thousand Faces.* Cleveland and New York: Meridan Press, 1968.

Capouya, John. *Real Men Do Yoga: 21 Star Athletes Reveal Their Secrets for Strength, Flexibility, and Peak Performance.* Deerfield Beach, Fla.: Health Communications, 2003

Chopra, Deepak. *The Seven Spiritual Laws of Success: A Practical Guide to the Fulfillment of Your Dreams.* San Rafael: Amber-Allen Publishing, 1994.

Baptiste, Baron. *Journey into Power: How to Sculpt Your Ideal Body, Free Your True Self, and Transform Your Life with Yoga.* New York: Simon & Schuster, 2002.

Baptiste, Baron. *40 Days to Personal Revolution: A Breakthrough Program to Radically Change Your*

Body and Awaken the Sacred within Your Soul. New York: Simon & Schuster, 2004.

Cantrell, Bridget C. and Chuck Dean. *Down Range: To Iraq and Back*. Seattle: WordSmith Publishing, 2005.

Curtiss, Harriette Augusta and F. Homer Curtiss. *The Key of Destiny*. San Bernardino, Calif.: Borgo Press, 1983.

Decoz, Hans. *Numerology: The Key to Your Inner Self*. New York: Perigree, 2002.

Iyengar, B. K. S. *Light on Yoga*. New York: Schocken Books, 1966.

Kumar, Nitin. "Om." *Exotic India*. http://www.exoticindiaart.com/article/om/

Manafort, Suzanne and Daniel J. Libby, PhD. *Mindful Yoga Therapy for Veterans Coping with Trauma*. Conn.: Veterans Yoga Project, 2012.

Maulana Karenga. *Kwanzaa: A Celebration of Family, Community and Culture*. Los Angeles: University of Sankore Press, 2008.

Millman, Dan. *Way of the Peaceful Warrior*. Tiburon, Calif.: H. J. Kramer, Inc., 1980.

Pinkola Estés, Clarissa. *Women Who Run with the Wolves: Myths and Stories of the Wild Woman Archetype*. New York: Ballantine Books, 1996.

Ruiz, Miguel. *The Four Agreements: A Practical Guide to Personal Freedom*. San Rafael, Calif.: Amber-Allen Publishing, 1997.

Salbi, Zainab. *The Other Side of War: Women's Stories of Survival and Hope*. Washington, D.C.: National Geographic, 2006.

Swenson, David. *Ashtanga Yoga: The Practice Manual.* Houston, Texas: Ashtanga Yoga Productions, 1999.

Tick, Edward. *War and the Soul: Healing Our Nation's Veterans from Post-Traumatic Stress Disorder.* Wheaton, Ill.: Quest Books, 2005.

Tolle, Eckhart. *A New Earth: Awakening to Your Life's Purpose.* New York: Plume, 2005.

Tolle, Eckhart. *The Power of Now: A Guide to Spiritual Enlightenment.* Novato, California: New World Library, 1999.

Yogananda, Paramahansa. *Autobiography of a Yogi.* New York: Perigree, 2002.

Williamson, Marianne. *Everyday Grace: Having Hope, Finding Forgiveness, and Making Miracles.* New York: Riverhead Books, 2002.

Williamson, Marianne. *A Return to Love: Reflections on the Principles of a Course in Miracles.* New York: HarperCollins, 2002.

Resources

SOLDIER'S heart

500 Federal Street Suite 303, Troy, NY 12180
518-274-0905
www.soldiersheart.net

TRANSFORMING OUR COMMUNITIES TO HEAL OUR VETERANS

Edward Tick, Ph.D.
Author, *War and the Soul*

There is a necessary, proper and reciprocal relationship between any society and its warriors. Our warriors willingly go into harm's way in order to preserve and protect the rest of us. In response, we must provide everything they need in order to return, recover and be restored to full functioning and life. They gave all; so must we.

War wounds and distorts our thinking, feeling, perceiving, our aesthetics, intimacy and sexuality, or will and concentration, our participation in society. War wounds every function ever attributed to the soul. Socrates taught that the soul is the seat of morality. Many veterans are anguished over what they have seen or done, and what has been done to them both abroad and at home. Thus, Post-traumatic Stress Disorder is a soul sickness. The acronym PTSD could be translated Post-terror Soul Distress.

PTSD unfolds in the public social sphere as well as in the private psychological one. In order to pursue war and keep the public supportive, governmental leaders and society in general deny the pain and suffering war causes and refuse to take responsibility for it. In any healthy society, there is a proper reciprocal relationship between warriors and civilians. During threat, warriors encircle and protect the rest of us. When they return, it is our responsibility to encircle and protect and tend them.

Instead, today, our wounded and veterans are shuffled out of view and their care left to experts or agencies that are understaffed and ill-equipped to respond. PTSD is a social disorder of any society that makes its veterans serve in dehumanizing conditions then denies, alienates and marginalizes them, their stories, experiences and suffering upon return. The acronym could be translated Post-terror social disorder.

We must see that PTSD is not just an individual psychological or medical pathology and cannot be healed through medical strategies alone. Rather, PTSD is both a soul sickness and a social disorder.

This is not a hopeless situation. Lifelong suffering from PTSD is not inevitable and our veterans ache for hope. When we understand PTSD as both a moral and social disorder that we have unwittingly forced our veterans to carry alone, then the path to home and healing becomes clear.

Here is some of what PTSD asks us to do for our veterans:

- Offer immediate response to any soldier or veteran crying out in unbearable pain;
- Create gathering places for veterans in every community;
- Create religious services that bring veterans spiritual cleansing and comfort;
- Restore the true meaning, respect and celebration of Memorial Day and Veterans Day — close the malls and gather in our communities and cemeteries instead;
- Create religious, educational and therapeutic programs by which veterans can seek not just psychological help but spiritual healing, cleansing and forgiveness;
- Create safe havens that are not only shelters for homeless or addicted vets, but are houses of initiation where vets receive not just job and sobriety training but education, therapy, and rehumanization processes;
- Invite veterans into schools and community centers to educate our young to the realities of war and service;
- Foster programs in libraries, community and cultural centers where veterans tell their stories to civilians and civilians honor and help veterans;
- Create a Veterans Service Corps so that those who have faced life's ultimate tests can find meaningful ways to serve for life rather than collapse into disability:
- Pair elder veterans with new returnees, much as

Twelve Step programs do, so that returnees never have to be alone with their nightmares and despair,

- Create 24/7 hot lines and drop-in centers so that veterans can find immediate help when needed;
- Teach veterans creative and expressive arts so that they develop tools for self-expression that balance the destructive forces and experiences they have encountered;
- Create prison-based programs for the special needs of incarcerated veterans;
- Evaluate veterans in the criminal justice system for the impact of military service upon criminal activities;
- Create hospice programs for the special needs of terminally ill veterans and their families;
- Create reconciliation programs with those we have previously fought, and between veterans and civilians;
- Create restoration projects so that soldiers who had to destroy or kill can once again learn that they are good people who can preserve, create and build;
- Create community based support systems for spouses and families of troops serving overseas;
- Create community based support systems for families of newly returned veterans with preparation and training for living with PTSD;
- Recognize and support other at-risk groups, such as grandparents and boy- and girlfriends of overseas troops and returnees;
- Evaluate and re-create our military training system

so that we do not dehumanize our troops as we train and prepare them for soldiering;

- Train many more health and mental health workers in veterans' psychology and teach that it is different from normative civilian psychology and they must apply different philosophies and methods in working with veterans;
- Educate health professionals and the public to become familiar with the ways of warriors and war so that we overcome veterans' alienation and society's denial.

We could institute such programs for our veterans and their loved ones. There is a path home. Restoration to full functioning is a goal toward which our vets can and want to strive. We must not rest from our healing efforts until they are restored.

By understanding the true holistic scope of PTSD and providing our veterans what they need for healing and return, we could set a model for the nation and the world. We can restore the broken relationship between our society and its warriors. We can reduce the incalculable losses that result from war. We would help heal not just our veterans but our entire society. Wandering and wounded warriors need a tribe waiting to receive and heal them. If we are that tribe, they will come home to us. Healing our veterans heals us all.

Yoga Tip: Breathe In, Breathe Out.

Breath comes first in yoga. You can bring yourself into the present
moment at any time, by bringing your awareness to your breath.

Easy Breathing Exercise:
Sit at the end of a chair, with your feet on the floor, hip distance
apart. Rest your hands on your thighs, with your palms facing up,
fingers relaxed in. Close your eyes, gently close your lips, and soften
your jaw. Inhale and exhale through your nose, counting to five for
each inhale, and five for each exhale. Make the lengths of the
breaths the same - slow, long, calm breaths, in and out through your
nose. If thoughts come up, allow them to dissolve away, one by one.

Whether you have 30 seconds or 10 minutes, you can do this any
time and anywhere. You'll feel a sense of calm and peace from this
simple pranayama practice.

www.YogaAcrossAmerica.org

I'm a Soldier in the army of the Lord,
I got my war clothes on in the army of the Lord,
I believe I'll die in the army of the Lord,
I got my breastplate on in the army of the Lord,
I'm gonna fight until I die in the army of the Lord,
Ain't gonna be no turning back in the army of the Lord,
I'm a Soldier in the army of the Lord,
I'm a Soldier in the army.

Gospel Hymn

Online Resources

www.africayogaproject.org

www.ashtanga.net

www.baronbaptiste.com

www.bootstrapusa.com

www.connectedwarriors.org

www.dcoe.health.mil

www.exaltedwarrior.com

www.givebackyoga.org

www.honoringthepath.org

www.irest.us

www.marianne.com

www.offthematintotheworld.org

www.thepeacealliance.org

www.thereandback-again.org

www.va.gov (U.S. Dept. of Veteran Affairs)

www.veteransyogaproject.org

www.vetsyoga.com

www.warriorsatease.com

www.wtc.army.mil (Warrior Transition Command)

www.woundedwarriorproject.org

www.yogaacrossamerica.org

www.yogaforvets.org

www.yogahealthfoundation.org

www.yogawarriors.com

I have been a seeker and still am, but I stopped asking books and the stars. I started listening to the teaching of my soul.

Rumi

About the Author

Michele M. Spencer, an Active Reserve Lieutenant Colonel in the Army Medical Service Corps, has served her country since 1986. She is an Operation Iraqi Freedom veteran, a Registered Yoga Teacher, an Acupressurist, a Certified Personal Trainer, a Reiki Master, and a Global Sacred Activist. She holds a master of science degree in Exercise Science: Health Promotion. She has been featured on the Armed Forces Network, CNN, and NPR, and in the *Army Times* and *Health and Prevention* magazine.